Cooking
outside the box

Keith Abel

Cooking
outside the box

The **ABEL & COLE** Cookbook

First published in 2006 by Collins,
an imprint of HarperCollins Publishers Ltd
77 85 Fulham Palace Road
London w6 8jb

www.collins.co.uk

Collins is a registered trademark of
HarperCollins Publishers Ltd.

Text © Keith Abel, 2006
Main photography © Cristian Barnett, 2006

09   08   07   06
9   8   7   6   5   4   3   2

A catalogue record for this book is available from
the British Library.

Photographer: Cristian Barnett
(see acknowledgements for other photographers)
Food and Props Stylist: Felicity Barnum-Bobb
Designer: Nicky Barneby
Senior Commissioning Editor: Jenny Heller
Editor: Gillian Haslam
Assistant Editor: Kerenza Swift

ISBN 13 978 0 00 723070 9
ISBN 10 0 00 723070 2

Colour reproduction by Colourscan, Singapore
Printed in Great Britain by Bath Press

Contents

Autumn 114

Winter 164

Introduction

If you've bought this book thinking I'm somehow related to Delia Smith or have some "Fat Duck" palate for mixing bananas and worms, I want to come completely clean and apologise profusely. Someone in the marketing department obviously got carried away. With some basic dishes I am a complete failure, and even my 11-year-old Jessica continually trumps me in the toast, spaghetti and boiled egg departments.

But before you start clogging up the returns department at Amazon, or boycotting Waterstone's thinking you've been sold a dud, I do have one thing over most cooks in that I have spent the last 18 years of my life working with the finest organic farmers, cheese-makers and artisan bakers, who produce a range of beautiful and delicious food that makes your average supermarket look positively cold-war Russian. Furthermore, for all these years I've been responsible for choosing the weekly vegetable shop for some extremely talented cooks (and a few chefs) across Britain who were just a bit fed up with the air-freighted, plastic-covered, plastic-looking, and plastic-tasting, produce being offered to them after the demise of their local greengrocer. The challenge for me and for Abel & Cole has been to keep the variety of organic foods coming month in, month out and, as word has caught on, to show the less adventuresome cook (like me) how to prepare, store and cook all the wonderful food on offer in the UK throughout the seasons.

The farmers I work with deserve 100% of the credit for my cooking inspiration. They invariably have a hundred-and-one serving suggestions for their much-loved and much-nurtured produce. I wanted to pass these ideas and recipes on to my customers, and so began the Abel & Cole weekly newsletter with headlines like: "The thing in your box that looks like a brain this week is celeriac." And the great thing about our customers is that they have always reported back on what works and what doesn't, and often send in recipes of their own. So grew a great bank of knowledge which I am now sharing with you.

The Abel & Cole Story

In 1988, after two successful previous summers of degree-taking, I got cocky and failed the bar exam. I had escaped the rigours of study (or lack of it) for the comfort of a tent in the south of Spain in a very old VW Beetle (damn, now I'll have to change the bank password) with my new (and first) girlfriend Catherine Ciapparelli (Chippy to everyone, Mrs Abel to me). The tan was going well, the windsurfing was improving and I felt pretty chuffed having this gorgeous girl as my beach bunny. I had been there about three weeks when I put in the call to get my exam results from my most amusing friend, Jeremy. When he told me I'd failed I asked him to stop ****ing joking around. He wasn't, which meant I was in real trouble . . . and a lot of debt. I had the option of carrying on clowning around on the beach or doing the sensible thing by heading straight back to London, putting in two months' hard graft with the books, and resitting the exam. Naturally I chose the former.

Over the next few days, though, I resolved to go home and set up business flogging potatoes door to door, a profession I'd mastered earlier to pay for my vices at Leeds Uni. So the plan was hatched. On my return I borrowed some traveller's cheques from my big brother and roped my friends Jules Allen and Paul Cole and my Mum into joining me in my fledgling business. One night in the middle of September I pitched up with the boys, £200 and a posh accent to New Covent Garden market to buy a load of spuds. By 7am, they'd been hand-selected and packed; by 8am we were double-sausage, egg, chips and beaned; and by 6pm the whole lot was sold. We were cashed-up and home via the pub by 10. Up again at 2am with Jules and Paul picking me up wearing their permanent smiles and constant good humour.

A few months in and we had a fleet of complete wrecks doing the rounds with a handful of handsome Kiwi fellas at their wheels. We'd added free range eggs to our service (taking the total product offering up to two), and emblazoned our new motto: "STOP BREAKING YOUR ARMS AND EGGS" all over our vans.

I should probably mention that at this stage I had no idea what "organic" was. Indeed, I was rather sceptical the first time I was offered organic potatoes. Of course potatoes were organic, I thought, they're *vegetables*. A farmer I knew told me about this organic thing and encouraged me to ask my supplier at the time (a Kent farmer) to show me what he used to fertilise his crops and keep the pests off. I tried hard not to look too shocked when the doors to the shed were pulled back. It was like a laboratory, and all of those chemicals were being dumped on our food . . . not the kind of thing you'd brag about while flogging spuds door to door. I got hold of my

3

first organic potatoes and our sales pitch changed from "bakers or mashers?" to "with chemicals or without?"

Up until then, our main challenge had been getting people to stick their heads out of the door for long enough to ask us, "How much are they?" Now, people were genuinely interested. Like me, they were discovering for the first time the amount of sprays used on their food. They had a lot of questions to ask and we knew some of the answers.

By the time summer came we had a large handful of very cool customers buying our first mixed boxes of organic vegetables. Their enthusiasm gave us a great sense of encouragement; meanwhile they were also telling all their friends about us.

Over the next ten years we carried on doing what we were doing, trying to run the business in a fair and decent way, and being constantly amazed at how rare this was in the modern food industry. It seemed that all the supermarkets were inadvertently employing sadistic post-pubescent buyers whose job descriptions appeared to read: "Bully, use your muscle, humiliate and bankrupt as many farmers as you can. We'll always be able to find others. Use any techniques you choose, no matter how underhand – they won't be able to say a word against you publicly or we'll put them out of business. Make them pay for promotions and if you cock up your weekly order, no need to worry: just say the produce is not up to scratch and make them pay for you to throw it away."

The more I heard about this, the more I was encouraged to just sell safe, healthy, local organic food bought from people I got on well with, supplied to people I liked, by people I enjoyed working with. While great on paper it was a financial catastrophe! Regardless, I kept believing it would work and eventually manna from heaven fell down in the shape of the good friends and mentors, past and present, who I've been so lucky to work with. And, like all good things in our part of the world, if you are prepared to show that you're not a lightweight and stick to your principles, the great British public will support you. For the last five years, one big virtuous circle has grown. All the hard-working farmers who were prepared to help us in the first place (quite often getting paid very late!) are now sustainably getting on with what they do best without a gun in their backs, and our wonderful customers are telling their friends about this strange bunch of people with their yellow vans who answer the telephone without a script and deliver fabulous food that you have to cook yourself.

A brief ethical guide to help you enjoy your fruit and vegetables . . . and meat!

Christmas is currently celebrated once a year, but I'm quite sure that if the people who run most of Britain's food shops had the chance, they'd be lobbying to see if perhaps there could be a second official Christmas in June as well, or maybe even once a month. And if this plan were to go ahead, would we enjoy the whole thing as much? Well, the first year might be rather novel but I'm sure that after a few years, Christmas would lose its magic.

This is exactly what has happened with our food. Now that you can buy strawberries in January and "new season" lamb all year round, many people just don't know what's in season any more, or that food eaten in its proper season actually tastes better. The most common question I'm asked by fruit 'n' veg junkies is, "so, what *is* in season?" As I've tried to show in this book, each season has loads of treats to offer. Not only is that how and when nature intended them to be eaten, but they won't be forced up out of the ground synthetically or duped into thinking it's another time of year with costly heating that causes all sorts of environmental havoc. Most importantly of all, by eating seasonally you are able to enjoy things shortly after they are harvested, and as anyone who has ever had a vegetable patch or allotment can tell you, food flavour and time out of the ground are directly related.

Finally, a real bugbear of mine is the method by which this out-of-season produce gets onto the supermarket shelves: airfreight. A common misconception is that *all* produce from abroad is airfreighted, and this is not the case. It simply doesn't make business sense for the supermarkets to airfreight apples which can be grown locally and stored for use, or bananas which can be sent by ship and then ripened on arrival in our ports. What is therefore likely to be sent by airfreight is produce that is expensive, light, delicate – and from far away, obviously. Look at the labels in the supermarket – if out of season, your asparagus is likely to be from Peru, your prepared French beans from Guatemala, and your baby sweetcorn from Thailand.

There is one great big caveat to bear in mind, and it's an important one to remember before you start to think this is all too daunting: there is no need to be puritanical about eating seasonally. Just as the odd pint at lunchtime doesn't make me an alcoholic, so feeding my children bananas or tomatoes all year round (and heaven knows it's difficult to cope without tomatoes all year round) doesn't make me either a bad parent or an ecological outcast. The message is just that if you make a point of becoming aware of what's best when and how it was grown, you'll not only enjoy the flavour more, but over time the scales will tilt in the right direction for the environment, your health, and the welfare of the people who grow your food.

Cooking "My Way"

Cooking: *v.* **cooked, cook•ing, cooks**
To prepare food by the action of
heat, or to become ready for eating
through such a process.

Cooking has quite a broad meaning. There seem to be no rules in doing this cooking thing, nor is there any specific result apart from making something ready for eating. (OK, OK, unless you're baking, or making something French.)

Bearing this in mind, most of the recipes in this book use local produce and can be played with, added to, miss things out, chuck it in, a little bit of this, a little bit of that, oops that's going to be a bit spicy, I think it needs more wine, hey I think I need even more wine . . . You might end up with the odd disaster if you get too carried away, but that's what cooking is about – experimenting and trying new things. So you haven't got any carrots, use a parsnip! No potato? Try a swede. Substitute your heart out, it can be very rewarding!

Most of the time you can work on the assumption that . . .

- Spinach = chard = kale = pac choi = all the cabbages = dandelion leaves if you're really desperate

- Potatoes = swede = turnips = parsnips = Jerusalem artichokes = beetroot if you're feeling colourful = kohlrabi if you're in a box scheme (good luck finding it anywhere else!)

- Squash = pumpkin = sweet potatoes = parsnips again = carrots

- Rocket = watercress = young spinach = lettuce

- Leeks = onions = shallots

- Celery = fennel = celeriac

- Pears = apples

- Broccoli = purple sprouting broccoli = asparagus = peas = green beans = runner beans = broad beans = all the beans

Cooking is also about enjoying yourself in the kitchen and not taking it all too seriously. Don't stand in silence when cooking – throw on a CD and shake your booty! Sing out loud and embarrass the kids. Take off your clothes and throw on a pinny. Take off your clothes and don't throw on a pinny! (Mind the Aga . . .) They say the kitchen is the heart of the home, so make it the place where people want to be, make it fun, and share the experience with your family and friends.

If you think cooking is a chore, you must be doing it the wrong way . . .

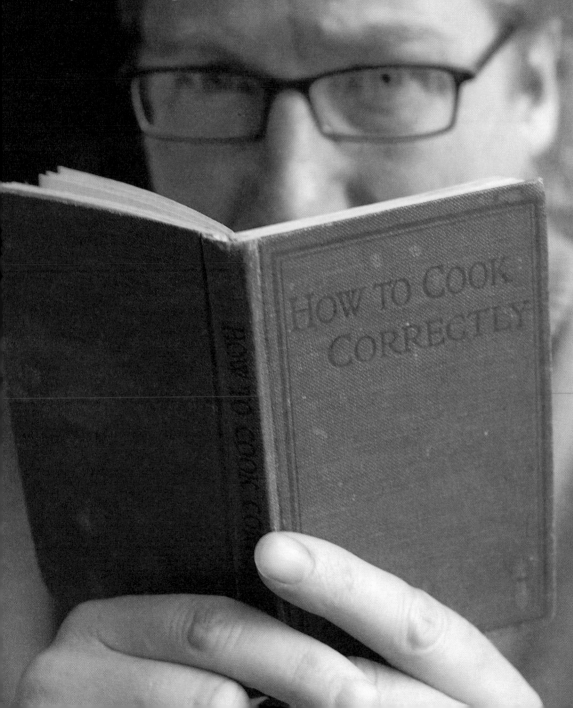

Knowing the slang

Cooking temperatures:

Most cooking equipment varies and has a complete mind of its own when it comes to temperatures. You know your own kit better than I ever will. If you have one of the following you will know what I mean: Aga, gas hob, electric hob, electric fan forced, halogen, ceramic, convection, hot spot, cool spot, top shelf, middle shelf, wood burner, oil burner, slow burner, kettle barbeque, gas barbeque, wood barbeque, camp fire, straight fire, magnifying glass. Nonetheless, here's a key to the temperatures in this book:

Farenheit (°F)	Celsius (°C)	Fan oven	Gas mark	Aga 2 oven	Aga 3 & 4 oven
350°F	180°C	160°C	Gas mark 4	Lowest set of runners in roasting oven, with cold plain shelf above	Baking oven
375°F	190°C	170°C	Gas mark 5	Lowest set of runners in roasting oven	Top of baking oven
400°F	200°C	180°C	Gas mark 6	Lowest set of runners in roasting oven	Lowest set of runners in roasting oven
425°F	220°C	200°C	Gas mark 7	3rd or 4th set of runners in roasting oven	3rd or 4th set of runners in roasting oven

A Warm Place

If you are lucky enough to have an Aga, there is normally a warming oven that you can use to keep things warm (obviously). Alternatively, if you have a double oven, turn on the lower oven only and put your food in the upper oven or grill section (the indirect heat of the lower oven keeps the top section warm). If neither of these options is available you can use the area on or around your cooker, making sure to pre-warm the plates or dishes and also to cover the dish with a lid or foil to keep your food from drying out. If all else fails, check where the cat hangs out – it's guaranteed to be warm.

The Griddle Pan/Ridged Skillet

This has to be one of my favourite pieces of cooking kit. When red hot, it becomes a sort of indoor barbecue that will not only give your food those great dark herringbone stripes, but also gives a wonderful smoky caramelised flavour. I know, it's not as good as a barbecue but let's face it, me standing out in the cold in the depths of winter barbecuing a nice piece of steak while Deputy Dog (my beloved labrador) is in the kitchen curled up in front of the Aga chewing on one of my shoes just doesn't cut the mustard!

If you haven't got a griddle pan already, be sure to get one that is made of heavy cast iron and be prepared to spend a few quid for a good one. It will last you several lifetimes and it might just end up being one of your favourite bits of kitchen gear.

Weights and measures. Or not ...

The Mug ...
... is the mug, every kitchen has at least one of them lying around and they pretty much all hold the same amount and they are always easier to find than the scales which you have buried at the back of your cupboard. In general, I think that's the best place for them, although I do ask you to get them out from time to time for baking and the like.

The Handful...
... is a sort of "go for it" sign, use as much or as little to suit your taste!

The Glug
See the splash

The Splash
See the dollop

The Dollop
See the glug

Once you get used to it, you'll love it!

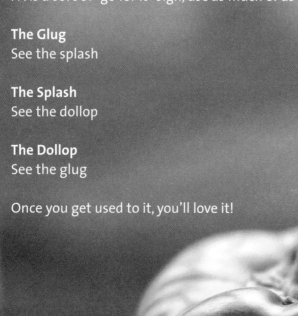

Spring

Having endured the British winter, the first days of spring really are a godsend. Only those who inhabit this wonderful island can appreciate what it's like to wake up when it's not dark, and enjoy the dawning realisation that the feeling on your skin is the sunshine that you haven't seen for five months. Then your last doubts are cast away when you see the beginnings of cherry blossom on the trees and the daffs opening up. It's time to dust down the Johnny Cash records again. Yep, the winter freight train just left town.

Unfortunately Mother Nature takes a little longer to recover from the months of darkness and damp in the fields. On the British organic farm, the overwintered crops planted in the autumn and grown all the way through winter start drying up. At the same time, the early-planted crops you're going to enjoy in the summertime are still unrecognisable little things battling for some soil alongside all the weeds. This is why the period from around March through until as late as June has been called the "Hungry Gap".

Maybe our forebears invented spring cleaning because there was bugger all going on in the vegetable garden and they couldn't watch *Little Britain*! This of course has many implications for the kitchen, so it's a great time for the seasonal cook to clear out the freezer and dust down the tins and packets at the back of the larder.

It should also be noted that the produce we do get through the spring is grown by the bold and the brave and I spend a lot of time traipsing around the country trying to persuade our growers to have crops ready for this difficult time. Small producers will have a much steadier bank balance if they grow crops in spring for the summer, rather than attempting to take Mother Nature head-on and grow things through the winter months for harvest over the Hungry Gap. Put yourself in their muddy boots: it's really difficult to stretch out the growing seasons without chemicals or sunshine and obviously if things go wrong they can lose the whole crop. So if your spring greens at this time are a little yellow on the outside leaves, spare a thought for the brave farmer who took the risk and grew them and enjoy them just the same.

Nonetheless, we need to be honest about this season: it's a tough one, but with a precious few delightful treats (like purple sprouting broccoli , rhubarb and curly kale) mixed in with the other produce that may need a bit of inspiration in the kitchen. So, as this is also a great time of year to use up those things at the back of the larder and at the bottom of the freezer, I've tried to include some dust-gathering favourites in this chapter.

Spring is the season for . . .

purple sprouting broccoli
asparagus
rhubarb
spinach
leeks
Jerusalem artichokes
carrots

Hearty Lemon Chicken Soup with Purple Sprouting Broccoli

This is a variation of the traditional Greek soup avgolemeno. The addition of purple sprouting broccoli gives the soup an extra burst of flavour and colour. Equally delicious with the chicken skipped and the stock replaced with a vegetable stock.

Heat the olive oil in a large soup pan over a medium heat. Add the garlic, onion and chicken and sauté until the chicken has turned white. Add the purple sprouting broccoli to the pan and continue to sauté for another 3 minutes. Now add the chicken stock. Cover and leave to simmer gently for about 25 minutes.

Remove the soup from the heat. Beat the eggs and the juice of one lemon together in a large bowl. Drizzle two mugs of the soup stock very slowly into the eggy lemon mixture, whisking constantly so the eggs don't curdle and it takes on a creamy consistency. (If you have some company in the kitchen, put your arms around them and get them to slowly pour the mixture while you whisk – so much more fun!)

Now gradually drizzle the egg and stock mixture back into the soup pot, this time stirring the soup constantly. Gently reheat the soup, taking care not to boil, then stir in the cooked rice. Add salt, pepper, and more lemon juice to taste and garnish with fresh parsley.

SERVES 4

1 glug olive oil

2 garlic cloves, peeled and minced

1 onion, peeled and chopped

400g (14oz) chicken, cut into bite-sized pieces

2 or 3 mugs of purple sprouting broccoli, cut into bite-sized pieces

4 mugs of chicken stock

2 eggs

Juice of 1–2 lemons

1 mug of cooked white long grain rice

Salt and freshly ground black pepper

Fresh parsley, for garnish

Lentil Soup with Red Wine Vinegar

VEGAN

If it's the night before your weekly veg delivery and things are looking a little grim in the bottom drawer of the fridge, you are now saved! Hallelujah for the lovely lentil!

Do experiment liberally with this recipe – I challenge you to find something that doesn't go well with it (except marmalade, I already thought of that myself). Leftover winter veggies, a tin of tomatoes and grated cheese on top will all complement it nicely. The red vinegar makes for a scrumptiously unique flavour and gives the soup an extra kick.

SERVES 4

1 mug of green lentils

1 potato, peeled and chopped

1 onion, peeled and chopped

2 garlic cloves, peeled and minced

1 bay leaf

½ tsp rosemary

4 mugs of vegetable stock

Salt and freshly ground black pepper

Red wine vinegar

Wash the lentils, add all the ingredients except the vinegar and salt and pepper to a large pot and bring to the boil. Reduce the heat and simmer, covered, for about 30 minutes – taste a lentil to check if it's done. If you want a thicker soup, remove the lid from the pot and simmer uncovered until it has reached your desired consistency. Season with salt and freshly ground pepper.

Place the red wine vinegar on the table so your guests can add as much as they like directly to their own bowls; 1–2 teaspoons per bowl will probably do the trick. Enjoy!

Chargrilled Asparagus and Halloumi with a Citrus Dressing

VEGETARIAN

If you're reading this recipe and thinking "I haven't got any pine nuts or halloumi cheese", turn to the Asparagus Risotto recipe on page 24 instead and relax. If you haven't got any asparagus either, phone for a pizza.

Pop the oven on 130°C/250°F/gas 1 and bung some plates in to warm.

First, whisk up the lemon, olive oil and parsley to make the dressing. Season with lots of black pepper and a little salt to taste.

Snap the woody ends off the asparagus (see the Asparagus Eggs Benedict recipe on page 22) and blanch them in boiling water for about 2 minutes. Drain and refresh in cold water. Then pat the asparagus dry and drizzle with a little olive oil to coat. Now cook for a few minutes on each side in a hot griddle pan, remove from the pan and keep warm.

While the asparagus is cooking, toast the pine nuts by tossing them about in a dry pan over a medium heat for about 2 minutes until golden brown. Watch them carefully to make sure they don't burn, and when they're ready, remove from the heat and put aside for the finished dish.

Now slice the halloumi into eight, brush with a little olive oil and cook in the griddle pan for a few minutes on each side until the slices have good dark char marks.

Make a loose stack of asparagus on each plate, top this with the halloumi and pine nuts and drizzle over the dressing.

SERVES 4 AS A STARTER

1 bunch of asparagus

2 tbsp olive oil

⅓ mug pine nuts

1 pack of halloumi cheese

The dressing:

Juice of 1½ lemons (use the remaining ½ for garnish)

½ cup olive oil

2 tbsp of chopped flat-leaf parsley

Salt and freshly ground black pepper

Asparagus Eggs Benedict

VEGETARIAN

As I crack open all the eggs that this recipe requires, I sometimes wonder if an egg farmer invented this dish. If so, good for him. Asparagus isn't compulsory of course, and pretty much any green veg will sit very happily between a softly poached egg and a muffin.

SERVES 2

12 asparagus spears

65g (2½oz) butter

4 large eggs and 3 large egg yolks

2 tbsp fresh lemon juice

¼ tsp salt

1 tbsp white vinegar

2 English muffins

Trim the woody ends of the asparagus or snap them off by just bending the stem end between your thumbs and forefingers until it snaps. Now you can simply steam or boil them until just tender, about 5 minutes.

To make the hollandaise, melt the butter in a pan until it's hot and starts to foam. While the butter is melting, put the egg yolks into a blender with the lemon and salt and give them a blitz. Now, with the motor running, slowly pour the hot melted butter through the hole in the top of the blender and keep it running until the sauce thickens (about 30 seconds).

Next, break each of the eggs into individual teacups. Bring 7.5cm (3in) of water to a light simmer in a deep-sided frying pan, then add the vinegar. Next, gently submerge the side of each teacup into the water and gently slide the eggs into the pan to poach for about 2½ minutes (for soft eggs which will be delicious and runny inside), then remove with a slotted spoon when cooked.

While the eggs are poaching, split and toast the muffins. Top each half with three asparagus spears, place the eggs on top with a slotted spoon and spoon over your warm hollandaise.

Asparagus Risotto

VEGETARIAN

This creamy asparagus risotto is straightforward – the asparagus does all the work for you. Use raw asparagus as a garnish for added texture and a fresh, clean flavour. Be sure to use only the freshest, British asparagus.

SERVES 2 AS A MAIN COURSE OR 4 AS A STARTER

1 onion, peeled and chopped

Olive oil

1 mug risotto rice

½ mug of white wine

4 mugs of simmering chicken or vegetable stock

1 bunch asparagus, about 15–20 spears, tough stalks removed

2 tbsp double cream

⅓ mug of grated Parmesan cheese

Salt and freshly ground black pepper

4 strips Parma ham (optional), for garnish

Follow the instructions for preparing the rice in the Roasted Squash and Wild Rocket Risotto on page 145.

Set aside the tops of a few asparagus spears for garnish. When you only have about 1 mug of cooking liquid left to add, steam the asparagus in a separate saucepan for about 3–5 minutes, until just fork tender but still with a bite.

Slice the steamed asparagus into 4cm (1½in) lengths and add to the rice when there is only a slight amount of stock left to absorb. When the rice is cooked through and the asparagus has been added, add the cream and half the Parmesan. Season with salt and remove from the heat.

Place on heated plates and top with strips of Parma ham and the raw asparagus spears. Sprinkle with the remaining Parmesan cheese and freshly ground pepper.

Wok-fried Sirloin with Purple Sprouting Broccoli

This is a great midweek supper and one of the many ways to enjoy purple sprouting broccoli – an English classic that had been almost forgotten for many years but is just starting to reappear on supermarket shelves, usually in cute little plastic-wrapped packs. We've been selling it by the boatload for years. Pah!

Mix all of the marinade ingredients together, pour into a glass dish, add the beef and put aside for half an hour.

While the beef is marinating, blanch the purple sprouting broccoli in boiling water for about 2 minutes. Drain and refresh under cold water.

Heat a couple of glugs of oil in a very hot wok, drain the beef from the marinade, reserving the marinade, and stir-fry the beef for about 1 minute. Add the marinade to the wok and continue cooking for a further 2 minutes before adding the broccoli. Cook for a further minute or so until the broccoli is heated through. Serve on warm plates garnished with toasted almonds.

SERVES 2 AS A MAIN COURSE WITH RICE OR NOODLES

The marinade:

1 tbsp soy sauce

A splash of dry white wine

½ tsp cornflour

½ tsp sugar

1 large garlic clove, peeled and crushed

½ a thumb of freshly grated ginger

The stir-fry:

2 beef sirloin steaks, cut into thin strips across the grain

2 mugs of purple sprouting broccoli, chopped into 5cm (2in) pieces

A couple of glugs of vegetable oil

The garnish:

⅓ mug of toasted almonds

Gazza's Goulash with Rosemary Dumplings

SERVES 6

The goulash:

2 glugs of olive oil

1kg (2¼lb) braising beef, such as chuck or blade, cut into 2.5cm (1in) chunks

2 large onions, peeled and roughly chopped

2 large garlic cloves, peeled and chopped

2 tbsp sweet Hungarian paprika (a very mild paprika)

2 tbsp tomato purée

4 mugs of chicken or beef stock, plus more if you need it

2 bay leaves

4 potatoes, peeled and cut into 1cm (½in) dice

Lots of salt and freshly ground black pepper to taste

Soured cream, to serve

The dumplings:

1 egg

½ mug of water

1 tsp salt

1 mug of plain flour

1 tbsp chopped rosemary

Gazza, aka Gazzman, aka Gary has been part of the furniture at Abel & Cole for almost as long as I have. He's also one of the coolest guys I've ever met, and he has the charisma to make whatever he's doing seem like the best thing in the world. Yes, even eating dumplings.

Heat a glug or two of olive oil in a large, heavy-based lidded pot, add the beef and brown it, then remove with a slotted spoon. You may have to cook the beef in batches so the pot is not overcrowded. Once the beef is out of the way, fry the onions for 3–4 minutes. Return the beef to the pot and throw in the garlic, paprika and tomato purée and give this a good stir around for a few minutes. Add the stock and bay leaves and simmer with the lid on for 45 minutes over a very low heat.

While the pot is boiling away, prepare your dumplings: mix the egg, water and salt together, and then add the flour, combine it and mix in the rosemary. Let the mixture rest for about 20 minutes or so.

Once the pot has been simmering for 45 minutes, add the potatoes and more stock if needed – you need the goulash to be quite wet for the dumplings to cook. After about 15 minutes, when the potatoes are tender, add the dumplings by dolloping one teaspoon of the mix at a time into the pot. Return the lid and leave this to cook for 10–15 minutes. Season with salt and pepper to taste and serve with a dollop of soured cream.

Hummus in a Hurry

VEGAN

This takes about 3 minutes from start to finish and tastes great. We always have a few cans of organic chickpeas in the cupboard just so we can whip this up as a healthy snack for the kids or even serve it up to guests while knocking back a few G&Ts before dinner.

1 can of organic chickpeas

1 large or 2 small garlic cloves, peeled and crushed

2 tbsp tahini (sesame seed paste)

Juice of a lemon (and another lemon for the G&Ts)

3 or 4 glugs of olive oil

A couple of pinches of salt

A couple of pinches of paprika

Drain the chickpeas, retaining some of the brine for later. Throw the chickpeas into a blender or food processor with the crushed garlic, tahini and lemon juice and start blitzing.

Slowly pour 3 or 4 glugs of olive oil in through the top of the blender with the motor still running so it all combines. You may need to scrape some of the mixture down the sides of the blender to get it all to combine. If it is too dry, re-blitz, adding a little of the brine to help it to loosen up to a smooth paste.

Season with salt and paprika to taste and serve with toasted pitta bread strips or sliced carrots.

Cauliflower and Three Cheese Comfort Supper

VEGETARIAN

Midweek easy comfort food. To make a children's version, just leave out the blue cheese and go easy on the mustard – unless your children are very sophisticated, in which case add some more (mustard that is, not children).

WILL SERVE 6 VERY HUNGRY PEOPLE

1 large cauliflower, cut into chunky florets

2 onions, peeled and chopped

500g (1lb 1½oz) dried short pasta, such as macaroni, penne or rotini

3 knobs of butter

3 heaped tbsp flour

2 mugs of milk

1 good dollop of hot English mustard

1½ mugs of grated strong Cheddar

½ mug of crumbled blue cheese (optional, ask the children)

Salt and freshly ground black pepper

½ mug of grated Parmesan

Preheat the oven to 205°C/400°F/gas 6.

Throw the cauliflower, onions and pasta into a large pot of boiling salted water and cook all together until the pasta is al dente, as per pack instructions.

While this is cooking, melt the butter in a medium or large pan. Stir in the flour to make a roux and cook for a few minutes, stirring over a low heat. Now turn the heat up to medium and slowly add the milk, constantly stirring until it all combines and starts to thicken to a creamy sauce – you may need to add a little more milk if it gets too thick and pasty.

Now stir in the mustard, Cheddar and blue cheese and season with salt and pepper to taste. Drain the pasta, onion and cauliflower and tip into a suitable-size baking dish. Pour the sauce over it and top with lots of Parmesan. Bake in the oven for 10–15 minutes or until the top gets nice and crispy, remove from the oven, serve and smile.

Spinach and Walnut Pasta

VEGETARIAN

This is comfort food that you can rustle up in 10 minutes when you get home from work or from something more fun late at night. Combining pasta water with the walnuts makes the sauce, and you end up enjoying the simple but delicious taste of walnuts, olive oil, spinach, Parmesan and seasoning. If comfort sounds like your idea of bland, though, fear not. Just chuck in some capers, sun-dried tomatoes or rocket instead of spinach, and you will be revelling in zingy refreshment instead.

Cook the pasta in a large pot of boiling salted water, as per packet instructions.

While this is cooking, blitz the walnuts in a blender or a food processor to a breadcrumb consistency and put aside in a bowl.

Add the spinach or rocket to the pasta pot 2 minutes before the end of the cooking time. Take a few spoonfuls of the cooking water from the pasta and mix it through the walnuts to create a paste. Add more water little by little until you have a sauce of the thickness you like.

When the pasta is cooked al dente, drain well and then pop it back into the pot. Stir through the walnut paste, the olive oil, half the Parmesan, the capers and the sun-dried tomatoes (if using). Season well and serve in hot bowls with the rest of the Parmesan sprinkled over the top.

SERVES 4

500g pack of wholewheat fusilli

½ mug of walnuts

2 mugs of finely chopped fresh spinach (or chopped wild rocket)

A glug of olive oil

½ mug of grated Parmesan

A handful of capers (optional)

A handful of chopped sun-dried tomatoes (optional)

Salt and freshly ground pepper

Spicy Purple Sprouting Broccoli and Sausage Pasta

This pasta topping is great on pizza too! If you don't have any sausages, you can always add another bunch of purple sprouting broccoli instead.

SERVES 4

400g (14oz) chunky pasta, such as farfalle

1 glug of olive oil

2–3 garlic cloves, peeled and minced

1 chilli, deseeded and finely sliced, or 1 tsp red chilli flakes

400g (14oz) sausages of your choice, sliced into 1cm (½in) pieces

1 bunch purple sprouting broccoli

Salt and freshly ground black pepper

1 handful fresh basil (optional), torn

Cook the pasta as per instructions on the packet.

Meanwhile, heat a large frying pan over medium-high heat and add the olive oil, garlic, chilli and sausages and sauté for about 5 minutes.

Roughly chop the broccoli, making sure to include the whole thing as the leaves, florets and stalks are equally tasty! When the sausage is cooked through, add the broccoli to the pan and sauté for another few minutes, until the broccoli is slightly tender, but still crunchy. Add salt and freshly ground pepper to taste. Spoon the broccoli and sausage over the pasta, sprinkle with lots of fresh basil on top and serve.

Variation: Try adding a glug or two of red wine to the sausages just before adding the broccoli. Let the wine cook down a little and then proceed as above.

Stuffed Green Pointed Cabbage

Not only are green pointed cabbage leaves the perfect shape for stuffing, they taste wonderful too. These may take a little time to prepare, but once they are in the oven you can chill out and take it easy for an hour or so. You can also try tossing in some dried fruits and any vegetables you have lying around.

Preheat the oven to 190°C/375°F/gas 5.

Blanch the entire cabbage so the leaves are just tender and peel away easily. Peel off about 16 leaves, taking care not to rip them. Cut out the thick stem and set the leaves aside while you prepare the filling.

Heat the olive oil in a heavy-bottomed frying pan. Add the onion, garlic and rice and cook, stirring, until the rice becomes translucent. Now add the lamb, herbs and spice, and cook for 3–5 minutes, until the lamb is browned. Finally, add the pine nuts, cook for a few minutes and remove from the heat. Season with salt and freshly ground pepper.

Line a heavy baking dish with any ripped or extra cabbage leaves. This will prevent the stuffed cabbage from sticking. Stuff the cabbage by placing the leaves on a flat surface with the inner sides facing up. Put about 1 tablespoon of filling in the centre of each leaf. Fold the leaf over the filling, first from the bottom, then the sides, and finally bring the pointed tip of the cabbage down to form a parcel. Place the parcel seam side down in the baking dish. Continue until you've stuffed all the leaves, making sure that the parcels fit snugly against each other. If the pan is too large, simply add a few extra leaves around the side as a cushion.

Mix together the lemon juice and chicken stock, and pour enough over the stuffed cabbage parcels to just cover them. Cover the pan tightly and bake for 1–1½ hours. If the stock evaporates completely during cooking, add a drop of water to the pan. Serve with a dollop of natural yogurt and garnish with dill.

SERVES 4

1 green pointed cabbage

1 glug of olive oil

1 onion, peeled and chopped

3 garlic cloves, peeled and chopped

1 mug of uncooked white long grain rice

450g (1lb) lamb mince

½ tsp dried mint

1 tsp dried parsley

1 tsp cinnamon

⅓ mug of toasted pine nuts

Salt and freshly ground black pepper

Juice of 1 lemon

2–3 mugs of chicken stock

Natural yogurt

Pinch of fresh dill

Beef and Pointed Cabbage Pie

I could call this "raid-the-pantry pie" sometimes! If we haven't got a can of tomatoes, I will use kidney beans, chickpeas, just about anything really. It's the same with the cabbage, spring greens, carrots, even the odd random parsnip. But at the end of the day, it always goes down a storm when it comes out of the oven.

First, boil and mash the potatoes for the topping. Set aside. Preheat the oven to 220°C/425°F/gas 7.

Heat a few glugs of olive oil in a large frying pan. Add the beef, onion and garlic and fry until the onion is translucent – don't move it around too much so you get some good colour on the beef.

Now add the cabbage and toss this through for a few minutes until it wilts down. Then throw in the tomatoes, including the juice from the can, the tomato purée and beef stock. Stir it all through and bring to a simmer. Add the Worcestershire sauce, and Tabasco if you're man enough, and let this simmer for further 10 minutes.

If the mixture is starting to dry out at this stage, add ½ a mug more of beef stock (or the dregs of an old bottle of wine) mixed with a teaspoon of cornflour so you end up with a gravy in the pan. On the other hand, if it's still very wet, just mix the cornflour with a little water and add this to the pan. Season with salt and pepper, check again that you've put in enough Worcestershire and Tabasco and pour into a suitable-size baking dish.

Top the mince with mash and cheese and bang into a hot oven for about 20 minutes, then finish under the grill for an extra-crunchy top.

SERVES 6

1kg (2¼lb) potatoes

2 glugs of olive oil

500g (1lb) beef mince

1 large onion, peeled and chopped

2 garlic cloves, peeled and chopped

1 small or ½ a large pointed cabbage, shredded, or use spring greens

1 can of tomatoes, chopped

2 tbsp tomato purée

½ mug of beef stock, plus more if you need it

A couple of good splashes of Worcestershire sauce

A splash of Tabasco (optional)

1 tsp cornflour

Salt and freshly ground black pepper

½ mug of grated cheese

Pan-Fried Chicken Breasts with Blood Orange Sauce

The sauce and the chicken take about the same time to cook, so this delicious supper takes about 20 minutes from go. Bookmark this page for when you've stayed at work (or in the pub) too long and have someone coming over.

This dish is fabulous with a pile of butter-sautéed spinach, or any greens for that matter, so don't forget to get them on the go as well!

SERVES 4

2 knobs of butter

1 onion, peeled and finely diced

1 tbsp flour

½ cup of white wine

Juice of 4 blood oranges

Salt and freshly ground black pepper

Zest of 1 orange

4 chicken breast fillets, skin removed

A glug of olive oil

To make the sauce, melt a couple of good knobs of butter in a medium-heated frying pan, add the onions and sauté until they are translucent. Now stir in the flour and pour in the wine and orange juice. Season with salt and pepper and let this simmer for about 10 minutes, stirring frequently, until it thickens. Finally, add the orange zest before removing from the heat.

Season the chicken breasts with a little salt and pepper and pan-fry in a little olive oil for about 5 minutes per side in a medium-heated pan, or until just cooked through and the juices run clear. Alternatively, you could cook them under the grill until cooked through. Once cooked, let them rest for about 5 minutes and then carve diagonally across the grain into four or five pieces.

On warm plates, serve the chicken slightly splayed out like you would put down a good hand of playing cards and drizzle with the orange sauce.

Stir-Fried Chicken with Radish, Chilli and Lime

Some things don't need introducing . . . serve with rice or in fajitas with a dollop of yogurt and garnish with radish leaves.

SERVES 4

6 large skinless and boneless chicken thighs, cut into 2.5cm (1in) pieces

Juice of 2 limes

Salt and freshly ground black pepper

1 red chilli, deseeded and finely chopped

A few glugs of olive oil

½ mug of chicken stock

6 spring onions, trimmed and finely chopped

A bunch of radishes, trimmed, halved and sliced

Grated zest of 1 lime

A handful of chopped fresh coriander or 1 tbsp dried

natural yogurt, to serve

A handful of radish leaves, chopped, to garnish

Start by marinating the chicken pieces in the juice of one lime, a little salt and pepper and the chilli for about 15 minutes.

Heat the olive oil in a hot wok or deep-sided frying pan, throw in the chicken with the marinade and stir-fry for about 2–3 minutes until the chicken takes on a little colour. Add the stock and spring onions and cook for 2–3 minutes until the stock has all but disappeared. Add the radishes, lime zest, coriander, juice of the other lime, salt and pepper and toss through for another minute, making sure the chicken is cooked through.

Heekerbeeker Kedgeree

This is named after the Heeks family, whose daughter Ella runs my business with me. Ella's mama lovingly developed this kedgeree over many years. It started off as a child-friendly version with a lovely creamy sauce, which the Heeks girls grew up with, and has gradually evolved into this more sophisticated, spicy version, like the grown-up daughters. I must admit that it's really rather light on vegetables, but everyone needs a day off sometimes.

SERVES 6

1kg (2¼lb) undyed smoked haddock

Bay leaves

Butter – anything from 25g (1oz) to a huge quantity, depending how your arteries are feeling

1 leek, chopped quite finely

5 tsp mild curry powder

A handful of sultanas

1½ mugs of rice

4 eggs

1½ mugs of frozen peas

2 lemons – juice 1, cut the other into wedges

Optional but very good:

Bunch of parsley

1 mug of whole roasted almonds

8–12 scallops

Rinse the fish and put in a big pan, cover with cold water and throw in a couple of bay leaves. Bring to the boil and simmer for a few minutes until it is just cooked (when it flakes easily off the skin). Hoick it out of the pan (leave the water where it is), take off the skin, pull out any bones you notice, then keep it warm on a plate, covered, in a very low oven.

Melt the butter in another big pan, fry the leek and cook gently until soft. Add the curry powder and cook for a couple of minutes. Then add a handful of sultanas and the rice and stir around to coat with the deliciousness in the pan. Add 3½ mugs of water from the fish pan (or as much as there is and top up with normal water). Bring to the boil and simmer for 15–20 minutes or until the rice is cooked.

Meanwhile, hard boil the eggs for 15 minutes in boiling water, shell them and chop up. Keep warm with the fish.

Chop up some parsley if you want to. Cook the frozen peas and drain. When the rice is done, drain off any excess water and gently stir in the fish and peas and lemon juice to taste (I use it all). Stir in more butter if you like (I do). You can either stir in or serve on the side the boiled egg, and chopped parsley and roasted almonds if using. You should definitely serve with lemon quarters.

For a dinner party version, poach two or three scallops for each person. Just before eating, put them in barely simmering water with a pinch of salt for 3–5 minutes or until cooked through (open one a bit and check it's opaque inside), and use them as the garnish.

Bombayed Jersey Royals

VEGAN

The new potato has been bastardised over the years with the constant desire to fill the shelves all year around with the little mites. If you are confused as to what early new potatoes *should* taste like, start with the Jersey Royal. Never was a name more deserving!

SERVES 4 AS A SIDE DISH

3 glugs of vegetable oil

1 tsp cumin seeds

1 tsp mustard seeds

½ a thumb of ginger, peeled and finely grated

1 large garlic clove, peeled and crushed

1 red onion, peeled and finely sliced

1 tsp turmeric

1 tsp garam masala

½ tsp chilli powder, to your taste (optional)

Enough Jersey Royal potatoes for 4, scrubbed and cut into 2.5cm (1in) pieces

Heat the oil in a hot, lidded frying pan and fry the cumin and mustard seeds for a minute or so until they pop. Now add the ginger, garlic and onion and continue frying for a further minute before adding the turmeric, garam masala and chilli powder (optional). Cook for 1 more minute.

Now turn the heat down to low and add the potatoes to the pan. Mix in half a mug of water, put the lid on and continue cooking for about 10–15 minutes, stirring regularly, or until the potatoes are just tender. You may need to add a little extra water to stop them sticking to the pan as they cook. Add just what you need to keep the potatoes mobile in the pan, though, so they're quite dry when you serve them.

Braised Fennel

VEGETARIAN

It's tasty, it's easy and it's great with pork, fish or chicken.

Sauté the fennel in the butter for 5 minutes in a lidded frying pan over a medium heat. Add the stock, cover, and cook over low heat until tender – about 15–20 minutes. Sprinkle with cheese, season to taste and toss before serving.

SERVES 4 AS A SIDE DISH

2 fennel bulbs, topped, bottomed and sliced 1cm (½in) thick lengthways

A knob of butter

⅓ mug of chicken or vegetable stock

A handful of grated Parmesan cheese (optional)

Salt and freshly ground black pepper

Green Pointed Cabbage and Soba Sauté

VEGAN

Green pointed cabbage is a lovely domestic variety and is the first cabbage available in Britain every spring that hasn't been overwintered (that is, grown all the way through the winter months). This recipe is also delicious with any green or white cabbage, so if you'd like to make it later in the year, just substitute with any other variety. If you haven't got any soba noodles, don't panic – you can always serve the cabbage up on a bed of long grain rice (it's just as nice!).

Bring a pot of water to the boil for the soba noodles and prepare according to the directions on the packet.

Toast the peanuts in a dry frying pan over a medium heat for about 2–3 minutes, or until they have taken on a nice caramel colour. Be sure to keep moving them around so they don't burn, then remove them from the pan and chop them coarsely.

Chop the cabbage into 2.5cm (1in) squares by cutting it in half, slicing it lengthways and then across. Discard the tough stem and separate the leaves so they are not clumped together.

Pour a small glug of sesame oil into a large, heavy-based pan, place over a medium-high heat and stir-fry the garlic and cabbage for about 7–10 minutes, or until tender.

Whisk all the sauce ingredients together well and add this to the pan. Reduce the heat to medium. Now add the prepared soba noodles and toss these through the cabbage and sauce. Remove from the heat and transfer to a wide plate, top with the toasted peanuts and coriander, and put a dollop of ginger in the centre. Serve with soy sauce.

SERVES 4

The main bit:

250g (9oz) soba noodles

1 small or ½ large head of cabbage

Sesame oil

4 garlic cloves, peeled and sliced thinly

The sauce:

2 tsp sugar

1 glug of sesame oil

½ mug of mirin (rice wine) or sherry

2 glugs of soy sauce

The garnish:

1 mug of peanuts

1 small handful of fresh coriander, chopped

1 tbsp pickled ginger or 1 tbsp minced fresh ginger

Soy sauce

Andrew's Roasted Purple Sprouting Broccoli

VEGAN

Andrew and I were at school together back in the twentieth century, or was it the nineteenth? We've also worked together forever. Not only is life without him unthinkable, but he is also the most fabulous cook.

SERVES 4–6 AS A SIDE DISH

3 or 4 glugs of olive oil

A bag of purple sprouting broccoli

A good sprinkle of sea salt

Balsamic vinegar, to serve

Preheat the oven to 220°C/425°F/gas 7. Pour the olive oil into a large roasting tray and pop in the oven to heat up.

Wash and dry the broccoli. Remove and discard the woody stalks (most of the stalks can be eaten – just as well, as there are a lot of them!). Chop the rest into 10cm (4in) pieces and toss in the hot oil, season with salt and roast in the oven for about 10 minutes.

Serve with a bowl of lightly dressed pasta or just eat it on its own. If you like (and Andrew does, so there's a recommendation), drizzle over a little balsamic vinegar before serving.

Jersey Royal and Radish Salad

VEGETARIAN

This pretty salad is crunchy and soft, tangy and delicious. It's wonderful as a side dish, but works very nicely served alone as a light lunch. If you're reading this one evening and tomorrow finds you able to make it for someone, phone a friend. They'll be a better one after lunch.

There is no need to peel Jersey Royals as the skin is thin and tasty – just give them a quick wash. Boil the potatoes in a big pot of water for about 20 minutes or until tender when poked with a fork. When the potatoes are ready, drain and set aside to cool.

Meanwhile, crack on with the remaining salad ingredients and add these to a large bowl. When the potatoes are cool enough to handle, cut them into chunks and add them to the bowl. Whisk together the olive oil and balsamic vinegar, toss this through the salad and top with the torn basil.

SERVES 4–6

2 big handfuls of Jersey Royal potatoes (about 10–15)

1 mug of radishes, topped, tailed and quartered

1 mug of pitted black olives

2 tbsp capers, finely chopped

1 block feta cheese, crumbled

The dressing:

2 glugs of olive oil

1 glug of balsamic vinegar

Handful of fresh basil, torn

Raw Button Mushroom Salad

VEGETARIAN

This tangy salad is delicious with creamy pasta dishes or with a big hunk of crusty bread. Try it by itself or on a bed of fresh greens. Rather than washing mushrooms, just brush them off with a tea towel, toothbrush or clean paintbrush and then there's no need to use kitchen paper. Remember we each have an average of 144,578,905 organisms living on us at any one time, so don't worry too much about the soil on the mushrooms. Happy stomach, happy planet!

SERVES 4 AS A SIDE DISH

Juice of ½ lemon

Glug of olive oil

Salt and freshly ground black pepper

Large handful of button mushrooms

Parmesan cheese

Combine the lemon juice and olive oil in a deep plate and add salt to taste. Thinly slice the mushrooms and add to the plate, making sure that all the slices are coated with the dressing. Allow them to marinate for a few minutes. Now shave just enough Parmesan cheese over the salad to barely cover it. Top with freshly ground pepper and serve.

Variation I: If you have any fresh herbs sitting around, chop them finely and toss them through.

Variation II: For a different texture and flavour, try adding thinly sliced celery to the mushrooms, or even replacing the mushrooms entirely with celery.

Variation III: Mmm, if we vary this any further, we may as well rename the whole recipe!

Baked Spinach
with Cheesy Woosty Eggs

VEGETARIAN

This is really nice for a Sunday breakfast with roasted tomatoes and sausages, and easy enough to pull together even if you have a stinking hangover or have had your lie-in cut short by kids/pets/birds singing/ something much worse/something much better.

Preheat the oven to 220°C/425°F/gas 7.

Melt the butter in a large frying pan over a medium heat, add the onion and garlic and sauté for a few minutes until the onion is transparent. Now add the spinach and sweat this down for a couple of minutes until it has wilted. Grate the nutmeg over, season with salt and pepper to taste and take off the heat.

In a separate bowl, mix together the cheese and eggs and season with Worcestershire sauce.

Spread the sautéed spinach in a lightly buttered casserole dish and then spread the cheese topping over it. Bake in the oven for about 20 minutes until the top is sizzling and brown. If the top is not brown, finish it off under the grill and serve with absolutely anything for breakfast, lunch or dinner.

SERVES 4–6 AS A SIDE DISH OR LIGHT MEAL

2 large knobs of butter

1 large onion, peeled and chopped

2 garlic cloves, peeled and chopped

1 bag of fresh spinach, washed and chopped

A good grating of nutmeg

Salt and freshly ground black pepper

250g (9oz) strong English Cheddar, grated

2 eggs

A few good splashes of Worcestershire sauce (to your taste)

Kiwi Muffins

VEGETARIAN

It may surprise you to learn that Kiwi fruit grows like weeds in certain parts of Italy. And we get stinging nettles . . .

This recipe makes about a dozen muffins using a muffin tray or you could cook them in six buttered ramekins, serve them with cream and call them "Kiwi Puddfins"!

MAKES 12

The wet:

1 egg

½ mug of milk

2 tbsp olive oil

The dry:

1½ mugs of plain flour

1 tbsp baking powder

1 tsp salt

½ mug of sugar, plus a little to sprinkle on top

1 tsp cinnamon, plus a little extra to sprinkle on top

The rest:

½ mug of peeled and chopped kiwi fruit

Butter, for greasing

Semolina, for dusting (optional)

Preheat the oven to 220°C/425°F/gas 7.

Combine all the wet ingredients in one bowl. Combine all the dry ingredients in another and then nice and gently mix the two together. Fold through the chopped kiwi fruit.

Lightly grease a muffin tray with butter (or you could use soufflé ramekins), then dust with semolina. Spoon in the mixture, filling each hole about half-full. Sprinkle over a little more sugar and cinnamon and bake in the oven for about 25 minutes.

Rhubarb Bread and Butter Pudding

VEGETARIAN

Rhubarb, rhubarb on the wall, the most delicious plant of all . . . when cooked properly. Here's a great example of how.

Place the chopped rhubarb in a dish, sprinkle with a good handful of sugar and set aside for about 1 hour or so to soften slightly.

Butter the bread slices on one side and butter a 25cm (10in) square ceramic baking dish. Lay four slices of bread (butter side down) in the dish and spread over half the rhubarb, repeat, and finally top with the last four slices of bread.

Now whisk together the eggs, cream, milk, vanilla and sugar, making sure they are well combined before slowly pouring it all over the top of the bread. Grate the nutmeg over the top and put this into the fridge for about 1 hour to let everything make friends with one another.

Preheat the oven to 190°C/375°F/gas 5. Set up a bain-marie on the middle shelf of the oven – use a deep-sided roasting tray large enough to sit the pudding dish in, and pour in enough boiling water to come halfway up the side of the pudding dish. Let this cook away for about 1 hour until the pudding is set and the top is golden and brown. Serve with ice cream.

SERVES 8

6 stalks of rhubarb, topped, tailed and chopped into 2.5cm (1in) pieces

A handful of sugar for preparing the rhubarb, plus ½ mug for the wet mix

Butter

12 slices of white bread, crusts removed

4 eggs

1 mug of cream

½ mug of milk

1 tsp vanilla essence

Freshly grated nutmeg

Ice cream, to serve

Rhubarb Salsa, Rumba Styling

VEGETARIAN

I can't remember where I got this recipe from, and it's one that I have never written down, until now that is, so I guess it probably changes a little every year, just like my dancing style. But unlike the dancing, I think it gets better!

Delicious with roast meats.

Simply combine all the ingredients in a heavy-based lidded pot. Bring to the boil, then reduce to a simmer for about 10 minutes with the lid on. Simmer for a further 5 minutes with the lid off, stirring every now and then during the cooking process. Remove from the heat and taste to see if you want to add any more honey, rum or vinegar to suit your taste. Serve warm or cold.

SERVES 8 AS A CONDIMENT

3 or 4 stalks of rhubarb, topped, tailed and chopped into 1cm (½in) pieces

1 onion, peeled and roughly chopped

A glug of wine vinegar

A glug of dark rum

2 tbsp runny honey

2 garlic cloves, peeled an crushed

A pinch of chilli flakes

A couple of pinches of ground cardamom

½ mug of chopped dried fruit of your choice – raisins, sultanas or whatever you have

Spring Scraps

Unless your diet consists solely of ready-meals, and your fridge has never played host to a vegetable (in which case massive congratulations for buying this book!), you'll be familiar with the sinking feeling you get when you pull open the veg drawer only to be confronted by a lonely celeriac/cabbage/cauliflower – or even something that doesn't begin with c. Whatever it is, it can be enough to have you calling 999 for a chicken jalfrezi with pilau rice before you know what you've done. Abel & Cole has been helping customers through these moments in their lives for many years now and there are loads of ways to do it. Here are just a few . . .

Soup

You can combine virtually any spring veggies to make a great soup. It doesn't matter what you put in it, the principles are the same.

1. Fry the onion

2. Add garlic

3. Add the other veg (e.g. potatoes, leeks, greens, root vegetables) and fry for a bit. You can also throw in red lentils at this stage.

4. Tip on stock (plus a drop of milk for a richer soup, or a tin of tomatoes for a tomatoey one)

5. Simmer happily until the veg is tender

6. Add any quick-cooking bonus ingredients (e.g. chickpeas, pasta, tomato purée)

7. Blend if you want to (but not if you've added pasta, ick)

8. Season

9. Serve

10. Dollop on any toppings you like (e.g. grated cheese, blue cheese, toasted seeds)

The world of soup is one of wild experimentation, so please let yourself loose and do your own thing!

Juices

In spring, your leftovers are probably going to be things like cabbage, carrots, cauliflower, spinach. This is good news because most of these make great juices. Juicing is all about experimenting and having fun, and just seeing what works. Here are a few combos I like to get you started; to make them, just rinse off the veg and push all the ingredients through the juicer. These quantities will serve two.

The Popeye Punch

A small handful of watercress | 2 large spinach leaves | 4 carrots | ½ to 1 apple (optional)

Delicious, fresh-tasting and very green!

Radish Royale

4 radishes plus tops | Small bunch of parsley | 3 carrots | 1 apple

This one is nice and sweet and it's the same colour as Dale Winton!

Cori-flower

4 cauliflower florets | A handful of coriander | 4 carrots | 1 stick of celery

This one may sound a bit crazy, but it makes a really good, hearty juice. This is thanks to the cauliflower, which emerges from the juicer as a bit of a mush, but works really well mixed with the juice of the carrots and celery.

And if it's too late for any of that . . .

. . . buy yourself a compost bin – a guilt-free graveyard for the veggies that just won't do for human consumption.

Summer

Just as summer term is when the results of all the hard work of the academic year are reaped (hopefully), so it is out on the farm. I try to visit farms twice a year, once in the winter for planning and once in the summer for salivating! The summer visit is always a real treat. I can remember years back dragging myself down to darkest Devon or the depths of mid-Wales in "Smelly" (the ancient, brakeless Peugeot I'd bought from a chain-smoking minicab driver), sweating the whole way but being met by such beauty as I've only ever seen on British organic farms in the height of summer. Places like the Gees' Llanlyr farm near Lampeter that was farmed by Matthew Merton, Bernard Govier's beautiful farm near Crediton or Guy Watson's rolling hills in south Devon were always such a treat to visit having spent months stuck in my warehouse in Brixton.

All these places were just a mass of insects, birds, vegetables and weeds. Weeds aren't always bad, it just depends on where they decide to grow – in the middle of the field competing with the crops obviously equals bad. But on the borders of the field, where they form the perfect breeding ground for helpful predatory insects, they are an essential part of life on an organic farm. I remember being absolutely awestruck by these borders, which were so lush with wildflowers and buzzing insects – why were the edges of the "normal" fields I'd been visiting for years so bare by comparison? What on earth was being sprayed on those potato fields to suppress this abundance of life? The answer, of course, was lots of chemicals that were highly effective at killing weeds – and with the weeds went the bugs, and with the bugs went the birds, and with that went me.

The argument for "conventional" food is that it gives us cheaper food, but as was becoming clear from visiting these healthy organic farms, this was at some cost. I was really struck by how naturally all the organic farmers would pull things out of the ground, wipe off the mud and eat them there and then. Fair enough with carrots, but they did it with everything from broccoli to beetroot and, not wanting to be fussy, I would join in. The real quality behind these vegetables was just majestic. Not the shape or the condition of the skin or outer leaves, but just the smell and the taste. Selling this kind of quality was going to be a piece of cake, I thought.

Things have changed a bit over the years, and overall for the better. Matthew Merton has now teamed up with Tony and Richard Norman, and with farms in Pembridge, Herefordshire, and can sell his carrots, leeks, celeriac and sweetcorn ten times over, while Guy got so busy with his vegetable delivery business that he has very little to spare for us. I have many more farms to visit than I used to, but it's always a special treat to go back to the fantastic people who've been with us for years and who are slowly changing the way we Brits think about our food. There are absolute diamonds like David Catlin in Bedfordshire, who brings us 30-odd acres-worth of the best vegetables known to mankind each year, from celery to summer leeks; Jane and John Edwards and their two sons at New Farm in Wrangle, Lincolnshire, who send us beautiful caulis, January King cabbages and Desiree potatoes; and Anne Evans at Blaencamel Farm in Wales, who works tirelessly through the summer growing gorgeous cucumbers, cherry tomatoes and broad beans . . . to name but a few.

What's brilliant is that the principle remains firmly intact and is reaching an ever wider audience: great food must be paid for and if someone is going to do a dedicated job properly year in year out, they need to be allowed to make a living or they'll be forced out of farming.

Organic farming in the UK is a great success story; since 2000, the amount of certified land has increased more than fivefold. Even better is that people are increasingly buying that food from independent retailers and not from the faceless shareholder conglomerates who try to tell us everything in their store is cheaper. And it's great that so many people are now not only asking that chemicals are kept away from their food, but also that the people who grow that food should be paid fairly and have some autonomy and security. And preferably live down the road rather than a jumbo-jet flight away.

Summertime is the time to celebrate all this. There is so much sweetness and variety in what the summer fields can give us that you can eat 100 per cent simple, British food from mid-June all the way to the end of the year if you wish. With that in mind, we've put together lots of fun, easy recipes to celebrate this small victory against "Big Food".

Summer is the season for . . .

salads   tomatoes   herbs   cucumbers   strawberries   peas in the pod
green beans   broad beans   runner beans   all sorts of beans   courgettes
aubergines   sweetcorn   plums

Cucumber and Celery Soup

VEGETARIAN

A favourite of the Abel & Cole lunch club, this is very easy to make for 20 people, so why not spark up a lunch club at your workplace or invite lots of relatives over?

SERVES 6

1 knob of butter

1 mug of diced celery

1 mug of sliced leek

1½ mugs of diced cucumber, plus some more as a garnish for each serving

1 mug of peeled and diced potato

2 mugs of chicken or vegetable stock

Salt and freshly ground black pepper

A good couple of pinches of cayenne pepper

A dollop of natural yogurt, to serve

A sprinkle of chopped fresh mint, to serve

Melt the butter in a large pot and sweat the celery, leek and cucumber over a low heat for about 10 minutes, stirring every now and then. Now add the potato and stock and a little seasoning of pepper, salt and cayenne pepper, bring to the boil, then reduce to a light simmer for another 10–15 minutes.

Blitz the mix with one of the many kitchen gadgets you have lurking in the cupboard until it's smooth and check for seasoning again. Run it through a sieve if you have one or just serve in warm bowls with a dollop of yogurt and a sprinkle of diced cucumber and mint.

Spicy Aubergine and Mozzarella Bruschetta

VEGETARIAN

Brings a little piece of Italy to a Wednesday in June when it won't stop raining.

Mix the olive oil, minced garlic, chilli and seasoning in a bowl. Slice the aubergine thinly, add to the bowl and mix well.

Now grill or griddle the aubergine slices for about 5 minutes on each side until tender.

Brush the ciabatta slices with olive oil and grill until golden on both sides, then rub one side with the cut surface of the garlic clove. Now assemble the bruschetta by layering the aubergine on the ciabatta, placing the slices of mozzarella on top, and then finishing it off with the parsley.

SERVES 2 AS A MAIN DISH OR 4 AS A STARTER OR SIDE DISH

2 glugs of olive oil

4 garlic cloves, peeled, 3 minced and 1 cut in half

1 minced chilli or 1 tsp red chilli pepper flakes

Salt and freshly ground black pepper

1 large or 2 small aubergines

½ ciabatta loaf

1 ball of buffalo mozzarella, thinly sliced

1 small handful fresh flat-leaf parsley, torn

Baba Ghanoush

VEGAN

Otherwise known as aubergine dip! I normally double all the amounts below and have leftovers to pick on with celery sticks when I get home from work.

SERVES 6 AS A DIP

1 large or 2 medium aubergines

1 or 2 garlic cloves, peeled

Sea salt

2 tbsp tahini (sesame seed paste)

2 glugs of olive oil

Juice of a lemon

Pinch of paprika

Preheat the oven to 190°C/375°F/gas 5, then prick the aubergines all over with a fork.

To get a lovely smoky flavour into the flesh, char-grill them directly over a gas hob. Simply put the aubergine down as if it were a saucepan, right over the flame, and turn it frequently with tongs. Keep going until the skin blisters all over – this should take about 5–10 minutes depending on size. Trust me, this works, but for safety reasons please don't leave the cooking aubergine unattended! You may also want to open some windows as this process can be a bit smoky. (Even better, do this over a hot barbecue if you have one going at the time. If so, you can also wrap the aubergines in foil once charred and finish roasting them over the coals). If using the hob, transfer them directly onto a baking tray once the skin is blistered and bake for 30 minutes. If you want to skip the char-grilling altogether, just add 5–10 minutes onto the oven-cooking time. Remove the aubergines from the oven when the skins are all wrinkled and let them cool for 10 minutes.

Cut open the aubergines and scrape out the flesh, cutting any big chunks into small pieces. Discard most of the skin – although a few little bits here and there will add to the smoky flavour.

Mash the garlic with a good pinch of sea salt using a pestle and mortar if you have them (if you don't, just crush against the chopping board with the side of a rolling pin) to create a paste. Put this into a bowl with the tahini, olive oil and lemon juice and mix together until smooth.

Finally, add the aubergine, mash with a fork until it's all thoroughly mixed and check for seasoning. You can also do the mixing in a food processor if you fancy, though I prefer the chunkier version using a fork. Spoon into a serving dish and sprinkle with paprika and a drizzle of olive oil.

Serve hot or cold with toasted pitta bread or dollop some in your favourite sandwich.

Portobello Mushrooms Kilpatrick

This is a little twist on the wonderful Oysters Kilpatrick. I guess a little twist is a bit of an overstatement considering there isn't an oyster in sight!

These are great as a side dish, a starter or a snazzy snack. You can even poach an egg and pop it on top of the cooked mushrooms for a brilliant breakfast (just skip the lemon).

Melt the knob of butter in a frying pan over a medium heat. Add the mushrooms stalk side down and fry for 1 minute, then flip them over and cook top side down for about 2–3 minutes.

While they are frying, fill the tops with the diced bacon, splash over some woosty sauce and season with pepper. Remove the pan from the hob and put it under a hot grill to cook for a further 5–10 minutes or until the bacon is cooked and slightly crispy. Sprinkle the parsley over and serve on warm plates, drizzled with the pan juices and garnished with wedges of lemon.

SERVES 4

1 knob of butter

4 large Portobello mushrooms, stalks removed

4 rashers of bacon, diced

Worcestershire sauce

Freshly ground black pepper

1 tbsp chopped parsley

1 lemon, quartered

Grilled Chicken Salad with Raspberry and Walnut Dressing

The best way to make this recipe is to put all the ingredients on a tray along with all the utensils you'll need, then wheel the BBQ to somewhere you'd not normally think of: under a favourite tree if you live out of town, or why not try an old cemetery if you live in town? Townies may get some strange looks (or arrested!) but the meal will be unforgettable.

SERVES 4

The salad:

4 skinned chicken breast fillets

Olive oil

Freshly ground black pepper

Your choice of summer salad greens for 4 servings

The dressing:

3 tbsp olive oil

2 tbsp walnut oil

2 tbsp raspberry vinegar

1 tbsp runny honey

Salt and freshly ground black pepper

Prepare the chicken by lightly brushing each breast with olive oil and seasoning well with pepper. Grill these on the barbie or in a griddle pan until just cooked through, and put aside in a warm place to rest for 5 minutes or so.

In the meantime, whisk together your dressing ingredients and season – feel free to adjust the quantities of oils, vinegar and seasoning to suit your taste.

Plate up your salad greens into stacks. Slice the chicken across the grain into strips 1cm (½in) wide and place on top of the greens. Dress the salad and serve.

Fresh Tomato Salsa

VEGAN

Salsa doesn't only come in a jar! It can be whipped up in a second and used as a dip, a side dish, or like ketchup. I love it in a steak sandwich or dolloped on a burger, washed down with a nice cold beer!

SERVES 4–6 AS A DIP OR SIDE DISH

1 glug of olive oil

Juice of ½ lemon or lime

2–3 large tomatoes, chopped as small as you like

1 red onion, peeled and also chopped as small as you like

1 large bunch of fresh coriander, chopped

1 chilli (optional), deseeded and finely minced

Salt to taste

Combine the oil and lemon or lime juice, mix with the veg, herbs and chilli and season with salt. It couldn't be easier!

Calcutta Lamb Burgers with Radish and Yogurt Salad

I've never been to India except in my mouth! I'm so looking forward to actually visiting, and have been for years. Until then, I'll enjoy cumin, coriander, yogurt and all sorts of other delights in dishes like this which are so easy to prepare and cook.

For the salad, simply mix the ingredients together and season to taste.

For the burgers, mix all the ingredients together in a large bowl, then shape into four round burger-shaped patties. Heat a little olive oil in a frying pan and fry the burgers for about 3 minutes on each side, or until cooked to your liking (I like mine pink, thank you very much). Of course, if you've lucked out with the weather, whack them on the barbecue.

You can also serve this with Bombayed Jersey Royals (see page 44) or Abel & Coleslaw (see page 83) and lots of the radish salad on the side.

MAKES 4 BURGERS

The salad:

⅓ mug of natural yogurt

½ red onion, peeled and finely diced

6 radishes, topped, tailed and finely sliced

1 tbsp fresh lime juice

Salt and freshly ground black pepper

The burgers:

500g (1lb) lean lamb mince

½ red onion, peeled and finely diced

½ tsp ground cumin

½ tsp paprika

½ tsp ground coriander seeds

A handful of chopped fresh coriander

2 tbsp mango chutney (optional)

Salt and freshly ground black pepper

Stuffed Lamb with Feta and Olives

SERVES 6

2.5–3kg (5½–7lb) bone-in weight leg of lamb, boned and butterflied (yes, ask your butcher to do this and give him a tip – money that is, not a cooking tip!)

½ mug of crumbled feta cheese

½ mug of chopped black olives

½ mug of pre-soaked bulgur wheat (see method on page 103 in Tabouleh recipe)

1 handful of toasted pine nuts, or any other nuts

2 or 3 garlic cloves, peeled and chopped

2 handfuls of chopped fresh rosemary or 2 tbsp dried

2 handfuls of chopped fresh parsley or coriander or 2 tbsp dried

Juice of a lemon

Zest of ½ a lemon, grated

A glug of olive oil

Salt and freshly ground black pepper

Serve this with steamed kale, braised fennel, buttered Jersey Royal potatoes and a couple of good dollops of Hummus in a Hurry (see page 28) or a simple gravy. Omit the accompanying bottle of Burgundy and expect your guests to strike you off their Christmas card list!

Choose a leg of lamb that will suit the amount of people you are cooking for – this recipe will serve about half a dozen, but the quantities can easily be adjusted.

Preheat the oven to 180°C/350°F/gas 4.

The first thing you need to do is make the stuffing by combining all of the ingredients, except the lamb, in a bowl. Then lay the butterflied lamb down flat with the flesh side up and spread the stuffing over the top evenly and firmly. Roll the lamb back together – you can do this in a few different ways depending on how it has been butterflied, but you want to end up with a fairly tight roll without any straggly ends hanging out anywhere. Tie this up well with butchers' string (or gardening string. Oh, all right then, your children's shoelaces!) and place in a roasting tin, seam side down.

Season the lamb well with salt and pepper and bake for about 20 minutes per 450g/1lb plus 20 minutes for well done or 12 minutes for the cannibal in you. Remove from the oven and let it rest for 20 minutes in a warm place before carving nice thick slices.

Lamb with Courgette, Lime and Ginger

This only takes 20 minutes from start to finish and goes down a treat with basmati rice and a glass of Rioja. Ideal for days when you wake up at noon with that "Oh my God, I can't believe I invited people to lunch today" feeling.

SERVES 4

2 glugs of olive oil

750g (1½lb) leg of lamb, boned, trimmed and chopped into 2.5cm (1in) chunks, or use lamb leg steaks

Flour, to dust lamb before cooking

Sea salt and freshly ground black pepper

½ mug of red wine

½ mug of lamb or beef stock

2–3 courgettes, sliced finger width

A large thumb of ginger, finely grated

Juice of a lime

2 handfuls of dry roasted and chopped nuts of your choice – cashews or peanuts work well

1 handful of chopped fresh mint or use 2 tbsp of dried if you can't get fresh

1 deseeded and chopped chilli (optional)

Heat the olive oil in a large frying pan over a very high heat. Dust the lamb chunks in flour, add to the pan and brown on all sides. Don't overload the pan – you might need to do this in two batches. Season with a little salt and pepper, remove the lamb and keep to the side in a warm place.

Now add the red wine and stock to deglaze the pan, then add the courgette, ginger and chilli (if using). Cook for 2–3 minutes to reduce the glaze, then add the lamb to the pan for a further 5 minutes or so until the lamb is cooked through. Add the lime juice, nuts and mint, season with salt and pepper, give it a good toss and serve.

Rack of Lamb with Wilted Greens and Tomato-Mint Dressing

"Spring" lamb means that's when it was born and it'll only be ready for us to enjoy a few months later. If you're eating lamb in spring, it once had a New Zealand accent. British lamb is thin on the ground in early summer, but is at its best in July, August and September.

Arrange the lamb racks in a ceramic or stainless-steel baking dish, ready for the marinade.

Whisk the oil, mint, vinegar and mustard together in a small bowl to blend, and season generously with salt and pepper. Spoon one-third of the dressing over the lamb and turn to coat evenly. Reserve the remainder, stir in the tomatoes and put to one side.

Let the lamb marinate at room temperature for 2 hours or cover and refrigerate for up to 6 hours, turning occasionally.

When ready to cook, preheat the oven to 220°C/425°F/gas 7, and heat up a large frying pan.

Remove the lamb from the fridge, discard the marinade and shake off any excess. Sear the lamb well on all sides in the hot pan, then return it to the baking dish and bake in the oven until cooked. This can take between 15 and 20 minutes depending on how large the racks are and how you want it cooked. When ready, remove the lamb from the oven and let it rest in a warm place for 5 minutes or so.

While the lamb is resting, start wilting the greens in a large frying pan with a knob of butter. You may need to do this in two batches, depending on the size of your pan. Each batch should take only a few minutes at the most to keep some crunch in the greens. Grate in a little nutmeg, season, and place a pile of greens on four warm plates.

Now slice each rack into four chops and put onto the piles of wilted greens – they look great with the bones meeting up in the centre. Spoon over the tomato-mint dressing and serve immediately.

SERVES 4

4 x 4-chop racks of lamb, trimmed of excess fat

½ mug of olive oil

⅓ mug of fresh mint leaves, chopped

4 tbsp white wine vinegar (add more if you like your dressings nice and sharp)

1 tbsp wholegrain Dijon mustard

salt and freshly ground black pepper

6 ripe tomatoes, seeded and chopped (see page 95 for method)

Salad bowl of roughly chopped and washed summer greens, such as chard or spinach

Large knob of butter

Freshly grated nutmeg

Honey-Glazed Salmon Steaks

Yummy, yummy, yummy and I've got a flat tummy. Serve this with the Two-Way Asian Watercress Salad on page 92.

SERVES 2

1 tbsp balsamic vinegar

1 tbsp Dijon mustard

1 tbsp runny honey

1 garlic clove, peeled and crushed

Salt and freshly ground black pepper

Olive oil

2 salmon steaks

Mix together the vinegar, mustard, honey, garlic and seasoning in a bowl. Brush over both sides of the salmon and leave in the fridge for about an hour.

Heat a ridged frying pan to a very high heat, then rub it with a little oil. Sear the steaks for about 3 minutes on each side, turning only once. The fish is cooked if it flakes easily when lightly prised with a fork. The cooking time may vary depending on the thickness of the salmon steaks and how you like them cooked. Remove from the grill, brush with any remaining glaze and serve.

Lemon Sole with Wine, Toasted Almonds and Capers

Summertime really is best spent outside enjoying the long evenings. If this recipe takes you more than 15 minutes, you're taking it all too seriously or actually have all the ingredients! I normally find myself missing some ingredients, can do this in under 10 minutes, and play a mean game of table tennis.

Start by toasting your almonds in a dry frying pan over a medium heat for about 2–3 minutes, tossing regularly until golden, then remove from the pan.

Dust the sole fillets with flour. Then heat up a good glug of olive oil in a big frying pan over a medium heat and fry the fish for about 2 minutes on each side. Season with salt and pepper, remove the fish from the pan and keep in a warm place. Unless you have a gargantuan pan, you will probably need to cook the fish in a few batches – not a problem at all.

Once the last fish has left the pan, put the wine in the pan and crank up the heat. Let the wine reduce by half, then add the capers, lemon juice, lemon zest, butter and almonds and give this a good stir until the butter has melted. Now plate up your fish and spoon over the sauce, sprinkle with parsley and serve.

SERVES 4

⅓ mug of flaked almonds

4 lemon sole fillets

Flour, for dusting the fish

A glug of olive oil

Salt and freshly ground pepper

½ mug of dry white wine

1½ tbsp capers, chopped

Juice of ½ a lemon

Grated zest of a whole lemon

A large knob of butter

A handful of chopped parsley, to serve

Abel & Coleslaw

A barbecue just isn't a barbecue without the slaw, and with the added bacon, this one will knock your socks off. And let's face it, socks do look pretty silly under sandals.

SERVES 4 6

½ head cabbage, shredded

1 carrot, peeled and grated

3–4 spring onions, trimmed and thinly sliced

⅓ mug bacon, fried until crispy and chopped

Dressing

½ mug mayonnaise (see page 84)

1 tsp cider vinegar

salt and lots of freshly ground black pepper

Mix dressing ingredients together well and combine with the vegetables. Season with salt and freshly ground pepper.

Baby Spinach
and Strawberry Salad

VEGAN

A beautiful and delicious summer salad. For a milder flavour, you can
use rice wine vinegar instead of balsamic. A lovely Kiwi called Todd
introduced me to strawberries in salads. Unsurprisingly, he also liked
kiwis in his salads. He tended to grate raw beetroot over the top and it
certainly didn't do him any harm – every Friday night he seemed to be
at another customer's party in Notting Hill.

Mix together the dressing ingredients. Combine the spinach and
strawberries and top with the dressing. Sprinkle the pine nuts or
almonds on the salad and top with freshly ground pepper.
Easy. Done.

SERVES 4

4 large handfuls of baby
spinach

1 handful of strawberries,
sliced

Toasted pine nuts or
toasted almond slices

Freshly ground black
pepper

The dressing:

1 tbsp balsamic vinegar

3 tbsp olive oil

1½ tsp brown sugar

1 garlic clove, peeled and
finely minced

Basic Whole-Egg Mayonnaise

VEGETARIAN

There are a few recipes in this book calling for mayonnaise, so we thought we might as well give you a quick simple recipe for you to make your own.

Take note that commercial mayo from a jar will last for months in the fridge and home-made only a few days. Hmm, I wonder why? Remember that this home-made version contains raw eggs, which some people prefer not to eat.

MAKES ABOUT ½ MUG

1 whole organic egg, at room temperature

2 tbsp white wine vinegar

½ tsp salt

½ tsp dry mustard (optional)

½ mug of light olive oil

Pop the egg, vinegar, salt and mustard (optional) into a blender and give it a blitz to combine. With the motor still running, very slowly and a little at a time drizzle the oil in through the hole in the top of the machine until all the oil has gone and your mayo has formed.

Variation: You can also replace the vinegar with 2 tbsp lemon juice for a different taste. I prefer the vinegar myself.

And now that you've made the mayo, you can enjoy the five-star version of:

- Abel & Coleslaw (see page 83)

- Swede Chips and Mustard Mayo (see page 147)

- Tempura Sea Bass (see page 190)

SIZE: 00m

FLOCK:

TYP

SL. ✓

S.A.

ORGANIC EGGS

from a **real** farm!

ORGANIC

Foil-Baked Aubergine with Sesame Sauce

VEGAN

This is a bit of a cheat. It's not really a recipe, more what a cook would do if faced with hunger and an aubergine at the same time. I'm not a cook but here it is.

Tip: Use up any leftover herbs you have lying around by putting them on the top at the end.

SERVES 4 AS A SIDE DISH

2 aubergines

2 tbsp soy sauce

1/4 mug of sesame seed oil

1/4 mug of rice wine vinegar

1 tbsp sesame seeds

Preheat the oven to 190°C/375°F/gas 5.

Prick the aubergines with a fork and wrap them well in aluminium foil. Bake for about 35–45 minutes, or until cooked through and tender inside. The cooking time will vary according to the size and shape of your aubergines. If you're barbecuing, simply put the wrapped aubergine on the grill, turning occasionally.

In the meantime, mix together the soy sauce, oil and vinegar.

When the aubergine is ready, remove it from the wrapping and grill on both sides for a few minutes, until the skin is nice and crispy. Now slice the aubergine into rounds and drizzle the sauce on top. Sprinkle with the sesame seeds and serve.

Runner Beans
in a Simple Tomato Sauce

VEGAN

This handy dish serves six as a side dish or add pasta and Parmesan and it'll feed four as a main! They eat this in Turkey all the time.

SERVES 4–6

A good big handful of whole runner beans, cut into 2.5cm (1in) pieces

A couple of big glugs of olive oil

A couple of garlic cloves, peeled and chopped

½ tsp fennel seeds

6 tomatoes, deseeded and chopped (see page 95 for method)

1 chilli, finely chopped (optional)

A splash of red or white wine

Salt and freshly ground black pepper

A little sugar to taste (optional)

A good handful of chopped basil

Start by steaming the beans for about 2–3 minutes, or until just off-tender. Run cold water over them when you're happy with them, so they stop cooking.

Now for the sauce. Heat the olive oil in a lidded frying pan over a medium heat, add the garlic and fennel seeds and fry for 30 seconds or so (watch it carefully and pull it off the heat if you suspect the seeds are trying to burn). Then add the chopped tomatoes, chilli (if using) and wine. Simmer for about 20 minutes with the lid on, stirring every now and then. If the tomatoes start to dry out during the cooking time, just add a little more wine or water.

Season with salt, pepper and a little sugar to taste. Add the beans and cook for a further 3–4 minutes, then stir through the basil and serve.

Garlicky Broad Bean Salad

VEGAN

Try growing broad beans even if you only have a windowsill. It's lovely
to watch them grow, they're great fun to harvest and more fun to eat.
Plant in April, water regularly and harvest in August. If you can't be
bothered, I know someone who'll deliver them about 15 hours after
they're picked!

Remove the beans from their cosy pods and simmer them in salted
water for about 5 minutes. Drain and then run cold water over them
for 30 seconds or so.

Combine the salad ingredients together in a bowl and add the beans.
Mix the dressing ingredients together well and mix with the bean
salad. Season with salt and pepper to taste.

SERVES 4

1½ mugs of broad beans
(as broad beans like
plenty of pod space, this
means you'll need about
4 large handfuls of pods)

2 stalks of celery, diced

1 large tomato, deseeded
and chopped (see page 95
for method)

1 large handful of fresh
basil, stems removed,
chopped

A few sprigs of flat-leaf
parsley, stems removed,
chopped

The dressing:

1–2 garlic cloves, peeled
and finely minced

juice of ½ lemon

glug of olive oil

salt and freshly ground
black pepper

Two-Way Asian Watercress Salad

VEGAN

The name says it all! You can have this salad two different ways – cooked or raw. For the raw, you will need only one bunch of watercress and can skip the blanching. And try adding in a handful of raw grated carrot and/or sprouts.

SERVES 4 AS A SIDE DISH

2 large bunches of watercress (for the cooked one) or 1 large bunch (for the raw one)

The dressing:

Sesame seeds

1 tbsp rice wine vinegar

1 tbsp soy sauce

2 tbsp sesame oil

Heat a frying pan over a low heat and add the sesame seeds (no oil needed). In a couple of minutes, they will start to smell delicious and turn brown. When they do, tip them out of the pan so that they stop cooking. It's easy to burn the seeds, so watch them like a paranoid hawk and shake the pan about from time to time as they cook.

Next, blanch the watercress by pouring boiling water over it in a bowl and leaving it for about 30 seconds, then drain and squeeze out any excess water with your hands. Chop it coarsely. If you're using raw watercress, just jump straight to the coarse chopping bit. Mix the dressing ingredients together well and pour over the watercress. Sprinkle with sesame seeds and serve with some grilled fish and rice.

Sweetcorn and Feta Salad

VEGETARIAN

This salad has a sweet and salty flavour thing going on that's divine with barbecued meats.

A little tip: tomatoes don't enjoy the fridge – keep them somewhere cool and sit them in a fairly warm room when you're ready to devour them. As they get softer, they'll only get sweeter. In short, tomatoes want sharp knives, not cold fridges. Much more fun anyway.

Start by steaming the cobs of corn for about 10 minutes until the kernels are tender. Allow the cobs to cool for a few minutes before cutting off the kernels. You can do this by standing each cob on its end and slicing down its length with a sharp knife, keeping close to the cob to retain all of the kernel and repeating this all the way around.

Now mix the kernels with all the remaining ingredients in a bowl and season with salt, if necessary, and freshly ground pepper.

SERVES 4 6 AS A SIDE SALAD

4 cobs of corn, husks and silk removed

1 large tomato, deseeded and chopped (see page 95 for method)

2–3 spring onions, trimmed and thinly sliced

½ mug of feta cheese, crumbled or cubed

1 glug of olive oil

A good squeeze of fresh lemon juice (optional)

Salt and plenty of freshly ground black pepper

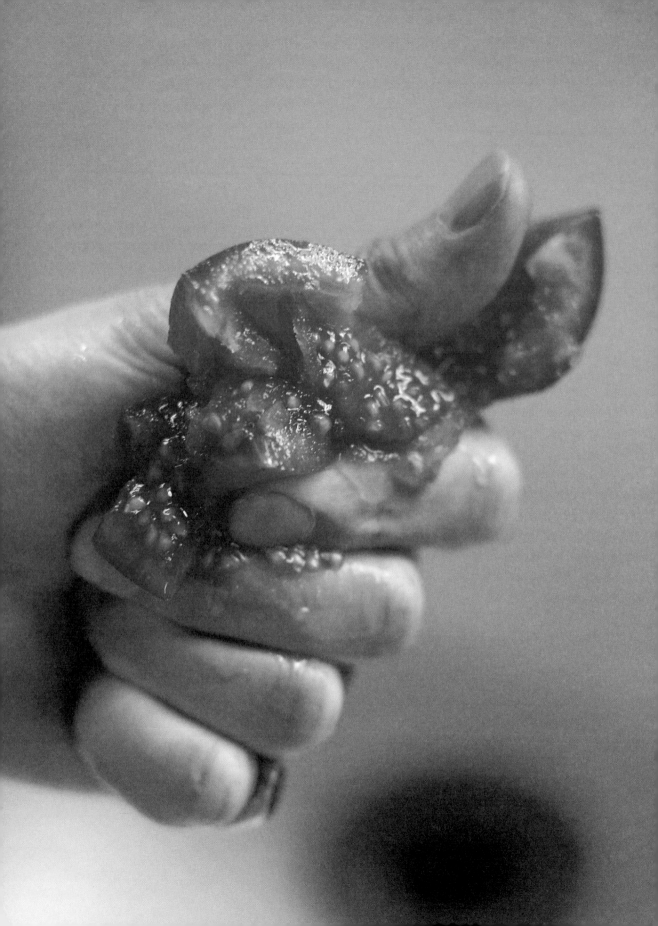

Squashed Tomato and Smashed Olive Bruschetta

VEGETARIAN

A simple recipe designed for Abel & Cole customers whose tomatoes have found their way to the bottom of the box. This makes a divine snack at any time of the year.

Make a small cut in the flesh of the tomatoes, then gently squash them in your hand over the sink or a bin to remove the seeds. Roughly chop the tomatoes and pop into a bowl.

Then smash the olives on a chopping board with a hard object, like a rolling pin, or if you want to look professional and have a steady hand, the side of a cook's knife. Remove the stones, roughly chop the flesh and throw the olives in with the tomatoes. Toss together.

Add a few glugs of oil, the oregano, a drizzle of vinegar, the chilli and the basil. Season to taste, and that's your mix.

Brush the ciabatta slices with olive oil and grill until golden on both sides, then rub one side with the cut surface of the garlic clove. Pile on the tomatoes and olive mix, drizzle with a little bit more oil if you feel like it and finish with shavings of Parmesan.

Variation: You could replace the olives with griddled or roasted red onion wedges (broken up a bit after roasting/griddling), which work equally well.

SERVES 4 AS A LIGHT STARTER

4 ripe tomatoes

⅓ mug of black olives

4 glugs of extra virgin olive oil

1 tbsp dried oregano or a couple of tbsp of fresh if you are impressive enough to have some growing in your garden

A drizzle of balsamic vinegar

A pinch of dried chilli

1 handful of fresh basil, torn

Sea salt and freshly ground black pepper

½ ciabatta loaf, cut diagonally into 1cm (½in) slices

1 garlic clove, peeled and cut in half

Shaved Parmesan cheese (a potato peeler does this really easily)

Stuffed Mushrooms

VEGETARIAN

Totally indispensable when you have a steak planned for the barbecue.

**SERVES 4–6 AS A
SIDE DISH**

**4 large handfuls of
mushrooms, any type will
do (except for the magic
variety!)**

½ mug of blue cheese

**Fried crispy bacon
(optional)**

**Freshly ground black
pepper**

**1 small bunch spring
onions, trimmed and
chopped finely**

Preheat the oven to 190°C/375°F/gas 5 or spark up the barbecue.

Remove the stems from the mushrooms, keeping the caps intact. Chop the stems and set aside. Now cut four large pieces of foil and divide the mushroom caps equally among these in a single layer, with their insides facing up. Tear off chunks of blue cheese with your fingers and stuff these into the mushroom caps. Now spread the chopped stems evenly on the stuffed caps, crumble over the bacon (optional), and grind plenty of black pepper on top.

Wrap the foil around the mushrooms, folding over the top to form airtight bundles, and place on the barbie or in the oven. Bake or grill until the mushrooms are cooked through and the cheese is melted – this will take 20–30 minutes depending on the variety and size of your mushrooms. If you're using a number of mushroom varieties and are concerned about the cooking time, or if you're using mushrooms like chanterelles which don't have defined caps, simply chop the mushrooms into chunks and crumble the blue cheese over the top.

When the mushrooms are cooked, remove the bundles from the heat, open them up and top with the chopped spring onions.

Summer Vegetable and Halloumi Kebabs

VEGETARIAN

When you know you have a vegetarian coming over for a barbecue, here's the recipe you need. After all, there are only so many veggie burgers and tofu sausages anybody can manage in one summer. These kebabs shouldn't just be reserved for the vegetarians, though. Serve them over some Tabouleh (see page 103) for a light meal, or enjoy them on their own. They also taste great cold the next day, so don't worry about making too many!

Make as much or as little as you like – eye up your quantities according to the number of kebabs you want to make. If you are feeling flush, reserve half of your kebab space for the halloumi chunks and just get enough veg to fill the gaps, but how much of each you use is entirely your choice.

Soak some bamboo skewers in water for 1 hour.

Cut some or all of the vegetables and halloumi into chunks about 4cm (1½in) square. Toss all the veg and halloumi in a little olive oil and the fresh rosemary. Now pop them all onto the skewers, alternating them piece by piece, and grill or barbecue until lightly blackened at the edges and tender – about 5–10 minutes on each side should do the trick. Remove from the heat and squeeze fresh lemon juice on the kebabs. Serve immediately.

Aubergine

Button or Portobello mushrooms

Peppers

Courgette

Red onions, peeled

Halloumi cheese (that magic cheese that doesn't run all over the place when heated and gets seriously delicious; oh God, you might have to go to the supermarket to get it . . .)

Olive oil

Handful of chopped fresh rosemary

Lemon, cut into wedges

Husk-Wrapped and Roasted Garlic Corn

VEGETARIAN

Unless you're planning on opening a restaurant, you can just call this BBQ'd corn! Did you know that two of the biggest predators of corn on the cob are badgers and deer? One Hampshire farmer we know goes out to his fields every night near harvest time to chase them off with his spaniel. So next time you go for a walk in the woods and see lots of old cobs lying around, you'll know there's been some kind of wildlife gathering!

SERVES 4 AS A SIDE DISH

4 corn cobs with husks still attached

2 large knobs of butter

1 garlic clove, peeled and crushed

2 tbsp fresh chopped parsley or soft herbs of your choice, such as dill, coriander or tarragon

Salt and freshly ground black pepper

The first thing you need to do is soak the corn cobs in their husks in water for 30–60 minutes to help prevent the husks from burning when being cooked. Then carefully peel back the husks and remove the silk from the cob, keeping the husks attached.

Mix together the butter, garlic and herbs and season to taste. Brush this over the corn and re-wrap the cobs with the husks, tying the ends up with butcher's string. (Normal string will also do the trick, provided it's made of natural fibres.)

Now you can either bake these in a 190°C/375°F/gas 5 oven for about 20 minutes or until the kernels are tender, or grill on a barbie for about the same time, turning frequently. If you're using a very hot barbecue, it's not a bad idea to wrap the cobs in aluminium foil to help stop the husks burning.

Tabouleh

VEGAN

This refreshing salad goes nicely with almost any meal and is especially good with Hummus in a Hurry (see page 28) and grilled lamb. In the UK parsley is generally sold in little bunches. In North Africa and the Middle East it is sold by the armful, and enjoyed with more abandon. Tabouleh is a parsley salad, so take a parsley leaf out of the Middle Eastern book and don't be shy with this wonderful green herb!

Put the bulgur wheat in a bowl or pot, pour the boiling water over it and cover. Let this sit for 20–30 minutes or until the wheat has nicely puffed up, then drain off any remaining water and let the wheat cool.

Mix the dressing ingredients together well and combine the dressing, chopped salad ingredients and bulgur wheat in a salad bowl. Serve and enjoy!

SERVES 4–6

The wheat:

⅓ mug of bulgur wheat

⅔ mug of boiling water

The salad:

½ cucumber, chopped finely

1 tomato, deseeded and finely chopped (see page 95 for method)

½ red onion, peeled and finely chopped

1 big bunch flat-leaf parsley, stems removed if you prefer, finely chopped – I like to include the upper parts of the stem as they add a nice crunch and it seems a waste not to use them

A few sprigs of mint, stems removed, finely chopped

The dressing:

Juice of ⅓ lemon

A glug of olive oil

Salt to taste

Fruit kebabs

VEGAN

One to make with the kids: you chop, they skewer, you cook, they play, you have pudding.

The fruit:

Melon

Plums

Apricots

Peaches

Any firm fruits are fine for this recipe, so the chunks don't fall off your kebab stick!

The marinade:

Juice of 1 lemon

Juice of 2 oranges or 1 mug orange juice

⅓ mug of brown sugar

½ tsp cinnamon

And, if you like . . .

A pot of natural yogurt

Nice vanilla ice cream

Some Honey Whipped Cream (see page 108)

Or why not all three

Cut a selection of some or all of the fruit into 4cm (1½in) not-very-square chunks, discarding any seeds or stones.

Whisk together the lemon and orange juice, sugar and cinnamon until the sugar has dissolved. (If you're making kebabs for a large crowd, just increase the amount of marinade.) Now pour the marinade over the fruit chunks and allow them to soak for about 10 minutes in a bowl.

Thread all the fruit quite tightly onto skewers, starting and finishing each skewer with the firmest fruit. Grill or barbecue for about 5 minutes on each side until the fruit is tender and the marinade has caramelised. Remove from the heat and serve with a big dollop of natural yogurt, a scoop of ice cream or some honey whipped cream.

Berry Soup

VEGETARIAN

The Finns love it for breakfast and I love it for pud!

Overripe berries work a treat in this dish, so if you haven't managed to eat all those English strawberries before they turned mushy, just turn them into soup! You can mix and match with all sorts of berries to get a great variety of flavours.

Put all the ingredients except the cornflour and sugar into a soup pot and bring to a simmer. Simmer lightly, stirring frequently, for about 20 minutes.

Now, mix the cornflour with a little cold water to dissolve it and slowly add it to the pot. You can adjust the amount of cornflour according to your desired consistency. Once the cornflour is added, check for sweetness and add sugar if necessary. Stir constantly for another 5 minutes, then remove from the heat. Berry soup is delicious chilled or warm. Serve with fresh cream or a dollop of yogurt and enjoy!

SERVES 6 AS A PUD (OR STARTER)

2 mugs of fresh or frozen berries, picked over

3 mugs of water

½ mug of organic blackcurrant cordial

3–5 tbsp cornflour

Sugar, to taste

Fresh cream or yogurt, to serve

Baked Strawberries with Honey Whipped Cream

VEGETARIAN

Health warning: this recipe only works with English strawberries in June. Do not attempt in February as the lack of taste may induce clinical depression.

SERVES 4

A punnet of English strawberries

A good knob of unsalted butter

3 tbsp sugar (use brown if you can – it's just so much more delicious)

½ mug of double or whipping cream

2 tbsp of runny honey

A splash of vanilla essence

Mint leaves, to garnish

The first thing to do is preheat your oven to 190°C/375°F/gas 5 and remove the tops from the strawberries.

Melt the butter in an ovenproof frying pan, add the sugar and give it a little stir before adding all the strawberries and tossing them to coat in the mix. Put the pan in the oven for about 5 minutes, then remove and turn the strawberries over and pop them back into the oven for a further 5 minutes.

While they are baking, whip the cream until it starts to peak. Then fold through the honey and vanilla and dollop evenly into four bowls. Remove the strawberries from the oven, place them on top of the cream and drizzle over the pan syrup. Garnish with mint leaves and serve.

Summer Surplus

Summer is the season for salad leaves, herbs, beans, peas in the pod, and soft fruits like berries and plums. Leftovers tend not to be an issue when the eating is as good as this, but if you do find yourself with anything that's lonely or past its best in your fridge, either sign it up to a dating agency or try some of these . . .

Smoothies

If you feel like a treat, the soft fruits around at this time of year will make fantastic smoothies. Here are some tips for smooth smoothies:

- As a general rule don't peel fruit as there are lots of great vitamins to be found under the skin, but you will need to remove the seeds and skins of thick-skinned fruits like melon and mango.

- Blenders work better if you chop things roughly first. If it's not blending very well, it probably just needs some liquid added. Water, yogurt, milk, soya milk, fizzy water, lemonade, left-over fruit juice, ice cream, spirits, liqueurs can all be thrown in! Don't be scared to experiment.

- Crushed ice really helps keep a smoothie smooth. If your blender is up to it, throw in a couple of ice cubes at a time as you make your smoothie. Otherwise, you can make slushy ice by putting some fruit juice or water in a shallow container in the freezer for about an hour and then giving it a stir.

- Don't forget the mini umbrellas.

- The art of the smoothie is all about throwing in whatever you find. Here are some ideas to get you started, though, all enough for two.

Banalon Breakfast

Yum. In your blender, throw together:

½ melon (peel, deseed and juice the melon) | 1 banana (roughly chop and blend with melon juice)

Wimbledon Smoothie

Ace. Blitz these together.

1 banana, peeled and chopped | Handful of strawberries | 2 apples (juice first and then blend with other ingredients) | 1 sprig mint (and more for the top) | 1 dollop natural live yogurt

Berry Blast with Mint

This is a great drink to use up any bruised berries left at the bottom of the bowl. The riper the berries the better – they'll be sweeter.

Squeeze 1 orange and ½ lemon and pour the juice into your blender along with:

Handful of strawberries | Handful of raspberries | Handful of red/blackcurrants (optional) | ¼ mug of cranberry juice | 1 sprig of mint

Tropical Blend

Throw on your straw hat, kick back and ignore all the washing up this one creates. You're on holiday now!

Squeeze the juice of 1 orange. Put 1 apple through your juicing machine. Then put the OJ and AJ in your blender along with:

½ pineapple | Handful of grapes (seeds out!) | ½ banana | ½ mango

Grapefruit Mary

I use a citrus juicer for this recipe on both the grapefruit and the tomatoes – it works just fine.

2 grapefruits | 4 tomatoes | Squeeze of lemon | Splash of Worcestershire sauce | Few drops of Tabasco (optional)

Mango/Cucumber Lassi

This one is as smooth as a baby's bum and goes a treat with a hot curry, cool as you like!

In the blender, combine:

½ peeled mango or large chunk of cucumber, cut into small pieces so it doesn't jam the blender | 2 dollops of natural yogurt | 1 sprig of mint | ½ mug of water

Decorate the top with mint to make it pretty and enjoy!

The Jade Garden

Tastes great – fresh and zesty. Lovely out in the garden on a summer's day. Make this one in the juicer.

6 kiwis | 1 cucumber | dash of lime

Apple and Vine breeze

Put this lot through the juicer and add some Pimm's to make a great punch.

2 apples | handful of grapes | large chunk cucumber | 1 sprig of mint (garnish)

Random salads

Summer is all about random salads. Just take anything that can be eaten raw, cut it up and you have a random salad. If you have only one ingredient, you can call it a relish instead. Shake up your own dressing in a jar (lemon juice, vinegars, mustard, olive oil, yogurt, crushed garlic, herbs are all good contenders). Just keep adding ingredients until you like it or the jar is full.

And if it's too late for any of that . . .

. . . bung it in the compost bin – the hot weather will take care of it super-fast. If you don't have a garden, ask a neighbour who does. Or invite a goat to hang out in your kitchen – they eat anything.

Autumn

When people talk about the autumn of their lives, I've never been quite sure whether they mean they are about to wither away and die, or whether this means they are finally freed from the day-to-day routine of full-time work and are now about to enjoy life with a bit of time on their hands and a bit of cash in their pockets. I suppose there are people who fall into both camps. Someone once told me life should really be the other way around, and if ever I become king of the universe I'll make it so that we are born as withered ancient beings with loads of experiences and slowly get younger (with the benefit of these experiences), eventually ending life as newborn babies.

With life being as it is though, when going into autumn we can either choose to consider it as the end of something (no more hot summer days and barbecues, and farewell to all those gorgeous summer fruits) or, as I prefer to think of it, as the beginning of one of my favourite times of year.

September is, without a doubt, the best time of year for British produce. It's also the only chance you'll get to gather some sloes and throw them in a bottle of gin to steep for a few months, thereby making silly games at Christmas a thing to look forward to and a lot more amusing.

October is your final chance to use the BBQ (if you're lucky), postpone painting the shed in the vain hope that the clocks won't go back, and wear that really cool shirt you bought way back in April when the sun first came out. It's also the last month you'll have to put up with southern hemisphere citrus fruit that doesn't taste of anything. Or if you've been sensible enough to boycott the supermarkets' obsession with stocking citrus all year round, it'll be time to set your tastebuds alive again with the joys of the Sicilian season.

In November you can finally light a fire, eat some game with British greens (the best in the world) and cuddle up to your partner without a layer of sweat sticking you together. Hey, even if you haven't got a partner, we all know we look our best in candlelight rather than on the beach. And my sister and I get to celebrate our birthdays.

Autumn is also a great time of year to be a British organic vegetable farmer. With all the really hard work behind you and having had only your early crops to sell to the handful of people who didn't leave the country in July and August, you now find your fields full of mature plants and gain the benefit of temperatures that won't start cooking the fruits of your labour 10 minutes after you harvest them. It's also a great time of year for the consumer to step out of the supermarkets and discover a whole universe of vegetables that don't normally inhabit their shelves (because they aren't sufficiently high-value to be flown in from all corners of the globe, and we all know that the big shops don't like to sell something that they can't stock 12 months of the year). This is produce grown here on our doorstep, ready to enjoy with only the need for a farmer, not an airline pilot – autumnal delights like Bright Lights chard, fennel with the flowers still attached and husk covered sweetcorn (without the cellophane wrapping).

Autumn is also the only time of year to be a British apple grower, although there aren't enormous numbers of growers out there to enjoy it. Amazingly enough, British apple orchards weren't wiped out by some virus that transmogrified the species barrier 20 years ago. Rather, at the height of what should be the English apple season the supermarkets are improving on the previous year's margin by selling left-over southern hemisphere fruit that's now as cheap as frozen chips because it's about to rot, hence forcing local growers to think again. The orchard keepers who were being paid below the cost of production for their fruit soon decided (or their banks did for them) that they'd be better off cutting down their trees, leaving their land to subsidised setaside and getting jobs that paid them more than their bus fare.

This sorry state of affairs is finally starting to change with the demand for locally produced food that hasn't had a chemical bath, and there are now some orchards with devoted farmers who are starting to scrape back a living – but only by selling those apples that are between 55 and 60mm across. I like to sell apples of all different sizes – small ones for the kids to get to grips with, big ones for my greedy self – and by getting our growers to send us a bigger range, we see them selling the vast majority of their crop, instead of just the medium-sized apples, and enjoying the fruits of their labour with a sensible income. And wow, don't those apples of whatever size taste fantastic.

Autumn is the season for . . .

squash • pumpkins • sweetcorn • beetroot • apples • pears • broccoli • leeks • spinach • kohlrabi

Pumpkin and Apple Soup with Toasted Seeds

VEGAN

This is a pumpkin soup with a bit of character. It's a bit like making a good risotto – straightforward if you read the recipe first. Needs a conversation with a friend or some music to help it turn out really well!

Other varieties of winter squash work nicely too. Try serving with the 45-minute Parmesan and Pumpkin Bread (see opposite) to follow – that way, if you have a large pumpkin, you can make a whole meal of it.

SERVES 4

3 English apples, peeled, cored and cut into 2.5cm (1in) chunks

½ large or 1 whole small pumpkin, peeled, deseeded and cut into 5cm (2in) chunks (keep the seeds)

A few glugs of olive oil

Pinch of chilli flakes (more if you fancy), or you could use fresh chilli if you like, or a pinch of powder

Drizzle of honey

1½–2 mugs of vegetable or chicken stock

Salt and freshly ground black pepper

A little crème fraîche (optional)

Preheat the oven to 220°C/425°F/gas 7.

Toss the apples and pumpkin in a few glugs of olive oil. Throw them into a roasting tin, sprinkle with the chilli and drizzle with honey. Bake in a hot oven for about 30 minutes or until the pumpkin is tender, turning it once or twice during the cooking time.

While the pumpkin is cooking, wash the seeds in a colander to remove the fleshy bits. Dry them on a clean tea towel and pop them into a medium to hot frying pan with a very small dash of oil. Shake these around for a few minutes or so, until they start to brown and pop. Remove them from the heat and season with a little salt.

Now put the contents of the roasting tin (scrape out every last bit) into a large saucepan. Add 1 mug of stock and simmer for about 15 minutes. Take it off the heat and give it a good blitz with one of those hand-held blenders, or use a food processor. Add more stock until you have the consistency you want for your soup. Season with salt and pepper, garnish with the toasted pumpkin seeds and a dollop of crème fraîche, and serve.

45-Minute Pumpkin and Parmesan Bread

VEGETARIAN

So you cheated on the soup and bought it in a carton (they are rather good these days). This is how you show your friends you're not a complete slacker.

Preheat the oven to 190°C/375°F/gas 5.

Mix the flour, salt, pumpkin, Parmesan, olives and rosemary in a large bowl. Now mix in the eggs and milk until they're combined and have turned into a sticky ball.

Drop this onto a greased baking tray to form a round patty. Grate some Parmesan on top and dust with flour before baking on the middle shelf in the oven for 45–50 minutes. The loaf is ready when you tap the bottom and it makes a hollow sound. If the top starts to brown too much before the bread is ready, cover lightly with some foil. Let the bread cool for about 10 minutes before serving.

MAKES 1 LOAF

1⅓ mugs of self-raising flour

Pinch of sea salt

1 mug of grated raw pumpkin or butternut squash

½ mug of roughly grated Parmesan cheese, plus extra for the topping

Handful of chopped black olives

1 tbsp chopped rosemary

2 large eggs, whisked

1 tbsp milk

Pork Loin Chops on a Bed of Sweet Orchard Apples

If I had one dream I'd like to fulfil one day, it would be to keep my own pigs in an apple orchard. But for as long as that remains a dream, I'll enjoy just cooking pork chops in this simple, delicious recipe. Fab served with any greens and roots.

SERVES 4

6 English apples of your choice

A few slices of ginger (optional)

1 tbsp sugar

2 tbsp cider vinegar

2 tbsp water

Juice of ½ a lemon

1 sprig of rosemary, stalk removed

Handful of sultanas (optional)

1 tbsp butter

4 thick-cut pork loin chops

Salt and freshly ground black pepper

Preheat the oven to 190°C/375°F/gas 5.

Peel, core and slice the apples and place them in a shallow baking dish. Add the ginger, if using.

In a separate bowl, mix together the sugar, vinegar, water, lemon juice, rosemary and sultanas, if using, and sprinkle over the apples. Cut the butter up and place it around the top of the apples.

Season the chops with salt and pepper and place them on top of the apples. Bake covered on the middle shelf of the oven for 30–40 minutes, or until the chops are cooked through.

Autumn Braised Lamb Shanks with Carrots, Parsnips, and Turnips

This dish is a great one for entertaining. Just prep it up, bang it into the oven and get chatting! A really honest dish to be enjoyed with good friends who don't need to be impressed by fancy cooking.

SERVES 4

4 lamb shanks

Salt and freshly ground black pepper

Couple of glugs of olive oil

4 garlic cloves, peeled

1 mug of carrots, peeled and coarsely chopped

1 mug of parsnips, peeled and coarsely chopped (or whatever root veg you have)

1 mug of turnips, peeled and coarsely chopped

2 tbsp tomato purée

1 mug of red wine

1 mug of chicken, beef or lamb stock

2 bay leaves

1 cinnamon stick

Chopped fresh thyme, to garnish

Preheat the oven to 190°C/375°F/gas 5.

Season the lamb shanks with salt and pepper. Heat the olive oil in a large, heavy frying pan and sear the shanks over high heat on all sides until well browned. Remove the browned shanks from the frying pan and place in an ovenproof casserole dish with a fitted lid.

Add the garlic and vegetables to the same frying pan and sauté for 3–4 minutes. Then add the tomato purée, wine, stock and bay leaves and bring to the boil. If there is not enough room for the wine and stock in the pan, just use the stock to deglaze the pan and pour the wine straight over the lamb in the casserole dish.

Pour the vegetable mixture over the shanks in the casserole dish and drop in the cinnamon stick. Cover and braise the oven for about 1¾ hours. The lamb should be fork tender, with the meat just beginning to separate from the bone. Let the dish cool for 10 minutes, then garnish with fresh thyme. Serve with your favourite mash.

Gardener's Chicken with Pumpkin and Walnuts

A really simple lunch. A gardening enthusiast friend of mine gave me this recipe to serve as a quick, wholesome dish to rustle up after a day in the garden, using just a few autumn vegetable basics (he grew his own, but you can get yours from me if you prefer).

Heat the olive oil and butter in a deep, lidded pan over a medium heat. Give the chicken pieces a good seasoning with salt and pepper and place in the pan, skin side down. Brown generously for 5–6 minutes, and then turn over. Try not to overcrowd the pan at this stage. You can brown the chicken in batches if need be.

Add the onion, carrots and pumpkin or squash and let these sizzle around the chicken for another 5–6 minutes, moving them around a little to catch the oil and butter. Now add the stock and pop the lid on, leaving a small gap to let the steam out. Let this simmer for around 30 minutes or until the chicken juices run clear when pierced.

Remove the chicken from the pan and keep warm. Add the sage and nuts. Turn the heat up and cook for a couple of minutes before serving up. Spoon the vegetables and juice onto the plates and rest the chicken on top before garnishing with the remaining fresh sage and walnuts.

SERVES 4

2 glugs of olive oil

1 tbsp butter

8 small or 4 large chicken pieces

Sea salt and freshly ground black pepper

½ mug of diced onion

1 mug of diced carrots

2 mugs of peeled and diced pumpkin or butternut squash (keep the seeds for Pumpkin and Apple Soup on page 120)

1½ mugs of hot chicken stock

Handful of chopped fresh sage leaves, plus some for garnish

½ mug of chopped walnuts or cashews, plus some for garnish

Roast Monkfish with Beetroot and Goats' Cheese Salad

Monkfish should only be eaten at certain times of year, when it's not spawning. Luckily, autumn is the right season, and it coincides with beetroot, which is the perfect complement to it.

Preheat the oven to 190°C/375°F/gas 5.

Start by washing and scrubbing the beetroot so it's nice and clean. Top and tail and cut into wedges or cubes (whatever rocks your boat), toss in a little olive oil and a good glug of balsamic vinegar, sprinkle the thyme over, season and place in an oven dish. Cover with foil and pop it into the oven for around 30 minutes. Now take off the foil and continue to bake for a further 15 minutes. Remove from the oven and set aside (but leave the oven on).

Now for the monkfish. Lightly season the fillets and place them in an ovenproof frying pan with a glug of olive oil on a medium heat. Sear on one side for 2–3 minutes, turn them over and bang the pan into the oven for a further 7–8 minutes.

While the monkfish is baking, build your salad on the plates – a small stack of greens and tarragon leaves in the centre surrounded by your beetroot pieces (keep the juice from the beetroot for the dressing). Crumble the goats' cheese over the top.

Now remove the monkfish from the oven and slice into finger-width discs. Place these on the salad greens, then dress the whole salad with a drizzle of balsamic vinegar, the beetroot juices from the oven dish, a little extra olive oil and a squeeze of lemon juice and serve.

SERVES 2

500g (1lb) beetroot

Good-quality olive oil

Balsamic vinegar

1 tbsp fresh thyme leaves

Sea salt and freshly ground black pepper

2 monkfish tail fillets

2 handfuls of any salad greens

1 handful of tarragon leaves

½ mug of crumbled goats' cheese, seasoned with salt and pepper and a squeeze of lemon juice

1 lemon, to squeeze

The Southwest Burger

No, it's not from Arizona. This peppery burger was inspired by the fantastic watercress grown in Hampshire and the tasty, tangy Cheddar we get from Somerset, hence the name Southwest Burger. The peppery watercress and beef is a fabulous combination of flavours. Bulgur wheat helps keep the burgers moist and light.

In a medium-sized bowl, combine the bulgur wheat with ⅓ mug of boiling water. Cover the bowl with a plate and let it stand for about 30 minutes until the bulgur is tender and the liquid is absorbed. Drain any excess liquid.

Now add the beef, watercress, onion, salt, pepper and Tabasco (if using) to the bowl and mix thoroughly. Shape the mixture into four thick patties and griddle or barbecue for about 5 minutes on each side or until cooked to your liking.

While the burgers are cooking, cut the ciabatta in half and toast it under the grill or on the barbie, then quarter it (why fiddle about toasting eight pieces of bread when you only have to toast two?). When toasted, rub raw garlic over the inside of the bread.

When the burgers are nearly cooked through, place 2 slices of cheese on top of each one, to give it a chance to melt.

Put your burgers on the ciabatta, pour on some of your favourite tomato ketchup and top with watercress.

MAKES 4 BURGERS

Handful of bulgur wheat

500g (1lb 2oz) lean minced beef

A couple of handfuls of watercress leaves, coarsely chopped (plus more leaves for garnish)

½ red onion, peeled and finely chopped

A few pinches of sea salt

A few grinds of black pepper

A few drops of Tabasco or other hot sauce (optional)

1 ciabatta loaf

1 garlic clove, peeled

8 slices mature Cheddar

Ketchup or other condiments

Wild Mushroom and Prosciutto Fettuccine

Pop into the deli (or better yet, farmers' market) on the way home and buy some prosciutto and a bottle of Chianti. Tell the other half you'll do supper or phone your nearest friend and get this ready in time for *Lost*, *West Wing* or, better still, *Curb Your Enthusiasm*.

SERVES 2 GENEROUSLY, OR 4 AS A LIGHT MEAL

2 large knobs of butter

1 glug of olive oil

3 shallots, peeled and finely chopped

3 mugs of wild mushrooms, brushed clean and roughly chopped

A few sprigs of chopped fresh thyme

100g (4oz) sliced prosciutto, roughly chopped

½ mug of double cream

Salt and freshly ground black pepper

3 good handfuls of fettuccine – about 350g (12oz)

Freshly grated Parmesan cheese

Chopped fresh parsley to garnish

First, make the sauce. Melt a large knob of butter with a glug of olive oil in a large frying pan over a medium heat. Add the shallots and sauté for about 3 minutes, or until softened.

Add the mushrooms and thyme and sauté for another 6–7 minutes until the mushrooms are golden, then add the prosciutto. Cook for another couple of minutes and add the cream. Let this simmer until the cream starts to thicken a little and season with salt and pepper to taste.

Meanwhile, add the fettuccine to a large pot of boiling salted water and cook it until al dente. Drain and transfer it to a serving bowl. Throw in a knob of butter and toss through before adding the sauce. Give it a good mix and serve with plenty of Parmesan and garnished with parsley.

Pumpkin Seed-Crusted Cod with Wild Rocket Salad

Cook this on the first Friday after Halloween when you're swimming in pumpkin seeds, and ask whoever you'll be eating with to pick up a bottle of Meursault on the way home. Tell them it's part of the recipe!

This will serve two people but just increase the quantities for more. And don't be afraid to experiment with the crust mix by using other seeds and herbs if you want to put your own stamp on it!

SERVES 2

2 thick-end cod fillets

Butter, for greasing

Sea salt and freshly ground black pepper

3 or 4 gratings of lemon zest

⅓ mug of pumpkin seeds

3 slices of 2-day-old bread of your choice

2 handfuls of roughly chopped flat-leaf parsley

2–3 tbsp olive oil

The salad:

Juice of ½ a lemon

1 tsp runny honey

1 tbsp good-quality extra virgin olive oil, plus a drizzle for finished dish

A couple of good handfuls of wild rocket

I medium carrot, grated

Preheat the oven to 220°C/425F/gas 7.

With a pair of tweezers (give them a good clean before and after and nobody will notice they were missing!), remove the bones from the cod fillets. Place the fillets on a buttered baking tray skin side down, give them a good seasoning and grate over some lemon zest.

Throw your pumpkin seeds into a food processor and give them a good blitz before adding the bread, parsley and a little seasoning. Whiz this until it turns a bright green colour before drizzling in the olive oil – you need enough just to get the mix to catch. (Do not let it get soggy in any way, or it will be no, no, no, to the chickens it goes!)

Now coat the top and sides of your fillets with the mix to a thickness of about 1cm (½in) and place them in the oven for 15–18 minutes or until the crust is golden and crunchy.

While your fish is baking, whisk the lemon juice, honey and olive oil together and toss through the carrot and rocket leaves. Make a small pile of salad in the centre of each plate for your fish to sit on.

When the fish is cooked, remove from the oven and place on top of each salad using a fish slice. Drizzle over a little olive oil and serve.

Mussels with Bacon, Leeks and Cream

I created this dish one night when I'd invited friends over for dinner. It all started by realising, ten minutes before cooking the classic moules marinières, that I'd forgotten Chippy had asked me to bring home some shallots or onions. After the panic had subsided and a lonesome leek was found in the bottom of the fridge, my plan was hatched and I pushed on to create something a little different!

In a saucepan large enough to hold the mussels, fry the diced bacon in a little olive oil until crisp, then remove with a slotted spoon. Now add the garlic and leek to the same pan with a knob of butter, and sauté for a couple of minutes over a low heat.

Pour in the wine and crank up the heat. Once the wine is boiling, add the mussels, stick the lid on and give the pan a little shake. Let the mussels steam for 2–3 minutes, until they have opened. Now remove them with a slotted spoon and discard any unopened mussels.

Keep the cooking liquid simmering for a few more minutes to let it reduce a little before adding a dollop of cream and the parsley. Spoon the mussels into bowls, pour the sauce over them and garnish with the bacon. Serve with crusty bread.

SERVES 4

4 rashers bacon, diced (any cut will do)

Small glug of olive oil

1 garlic clove, peeled, smashed and chopped

1 leek, washed and finely shredded

Knob of butter

1 mug of dry white wine

1kg (2¼lb) mussels, cleaned and de-bearded, open ones discarded

A dollop of double cream

Handful of fresh flat-leaf parsley, chopped

Plenty of crusty bread

Orkney Salmon Steaks
with Chard and Coconut Sauce

Sounds glam, but really this is not that difficult as long as you are partial to an occasional piña colada or Thai food and thus have coconut milk in your cupboard.

SERVES 4

4cm (1½in) fresh ginger

4 salmon steaks or fillets

Sea salt and freshly ground black pepper

Chard – about a handful when held by the stalks

A glug of olive oil

1 large onion, peeled and thinly sliced

4 tomatoes, deseeded and chopped

1 tsp sugar

½ mug coconut milk

½ mug water

Juice of 1 lime

1 handful of chopped fresh coriander

Slice the ginger and cut into slivers (it's not necessary to peel the ginger – just cut off any tough bits). Season the salmon with salt and pepper and set aside. Strip the chard leaves from the stalks and roughly chop the leaves. Dice the stalks into small pieces.

Heat the oil in a wide, deep frying pan over a medium heat. Add the onion, ginger and chard stems and cook, stirring occasionally, for about 5 minutes.

Add the chopped tomatoes and the sugar and continue to cook for another 4–5 minutes. Add the coconut milk and water and season well with salt and pepper. Stir, bring to the boil, then simmer over a low heat for a further 15 minutes.

Stir in the chard leaves, squeeze the lime over them and arrange the salmon pieces in a single layer over the top of the sauce. Spoon some of the liquid over the fish. Cover with a tight-fitting lid, return to a medium heat, and simmer for about 10 minutes, or until the fish is just cooked through.

To serve, lift the fish and chard sauce onto a hot serving dish. Spoon the remaining liquid over the top of the fish, garnish with coriander and serve immediately with rice.

Borlotti Bean and Squash Stew

VEGAN

This hearty stew blends the last crops of summer with autumn's first offerings, creating a dish bursting with flavour, colour and texture. Feel free to experiment with other fresh veggies. More likely than not, they'll work very nicely, and I can personally vouch for the suitability of peppers, courgettes and potatoes. You can also try puréeing some or all of the soup before adding the spinach for a different texture, or adding a hot chilli pepper for extra spice.

Simmer the borlotti beans in lightly salted water for 15 minutes, until just tender. Drain the beans and rinse. If you would like to use dried beans, make sure they've been soaked overnight, then cooked and drained.

Heat the oil in a large soup pot, add the onion and garlic and sauté briefly. Then add the salt, cayenne (if using) and oregano and continue to sauté until the onions are translucent. Add the squash and the vegetable stock and bring to a simmer. Simmer for about 10 minutes or until the squash is just tender. Now add the beans, tomatoes and corn and simmer for another 15 minutes, adding more vegetable stock or water if you prefer a thinner consistency. Add the spinach and allow to simmer for a few more minutes, until the spinach is wilted.

Season with salt and pepper, and garnish with fresh basil. A little freshly grated Parmesan or Cheddar cheese on top tastes good too. This soup goes nicely with dips and bread or a big, crunchy salad. It tastes great the next day too – and the day after that . . .

SERVES 4–6

3 mugs of fresh borlotti beans

Olive oil

1 onion, peeled and chopped

4 garlic cloves, peeled and minced

Salt and freshly ground black pepper

A couple of pinches of salt

A dash of cayenne (optional)

1 tsp dried oregano

4 mugs of peeled, cubed and seeded squash or pumpkin

4–5 mugs of vegetable stock

4 mugs of chopped tomatoes

2 mugs of corn kernels, preferably fresh, but frozen or tinned will work

4 big handfuls of spinach, roughly chopped

Chopped fresh basil, for garnish

Venison Sausages with Colcannon and Wild Mushroom Sauce

SERVES 6

18 venison sausages

The colcannon:

2kg (4½lb) potatoes, peeled and cut into 4cm (1½in) pieces

1 Savoy cabbage, cored and finely shredded

3 or 4 large knobs of butter

⅓ mug of milk (or more if you like)

2 or 3 shallots or a red onion, peeled and finely chopped

Salt and freshly ground black pepper

The mushroom sauce:

1 large knob of butter

1 medium red onion, peeled and finely chopped

2 mugs of wild mushrooms, brushed clean and roughly chopped

¾ mug of port or fruity red wine

2½ tsp cornflour

1 mug of beef stock

Salt and freshly ground black pepper

Don't be put off by the sound of colcannon – it's just Irish for cabbage mashed up with potatoes. This recipe is really bangers and mash with a fancy dinner-party name. It will feed six hungry hunters with enough leftover colcannon to make bubble and squeak the following morning. The colcannon traditionally has a well of melted butter floating on top; I think you will find a well of this mushroom sauce will do the trick just fine.

Boil the potatoes in a large pan of salted water for 10–12 minutes. Meanwhile, get the sausages cooking under the grill.

While the sausages and spuds are cooking, you can make the sauce. Start by melting the butter in a large frying pan. Add the red onion and sauté for 4–5 minutes, until starting to soften. Add the mushrooms and cook for a further 2–3 minutes. Season well, add the port or wine and cook uncovered for another 3–4 minutes to reduce slightly.

Mix the cornflour to a smooth paste with a little cold water and gradually add this to the pan. Bring to the boil, stir in the stock and cook for another 1–2 minutes or so, stirring constantly until the sauce thickens, then remove from the heat.

Add the shredded cabbage to the pan of potatoes. Cook for a further 4–5 minutes until the cabbage and potatoes are just tender. Drain and return the spuds and cabbage to the pot. Now add the butter, milk, and onions and get on mashing. Season to taste and serve garnished with whatever you can find around, together with the sausages and a good ladle of sauce!

Spinachio Pie

VEGETARIAN

People will eat as much of this as you cook, so if you wish, make 1½ quantities and use a 25cm (10in) dish. This pie is fabulous hot or cold. We eat it with roast potatoes and a tomato salad.

To make the pastry, sift the flours and salt together into a bowl. Rub the butter into the flour to breadcrumb consistency. Gradually add enough cold water (about 3 tbsp) until the pastry just sticks together. If you're being really posh, let the pastry rest for half an hour.

Preheat the oven to 200°C/400°F/gas 6.

Roll out the pastry and use it to line a greased 20cm (8in) pie dish or flan tin. Prick the base all over with a fork. Bake blind for 10 minutes.

While the pastry is baking, separate one of the eggs and whisk the white lightly with a fork.

Now, here's the wizard wheeze. Take the pastry out of the oven. Pour the whisked egg white into the base, swish it around until it is covered, tip any extra back into the bowl, then pop the pastry back into the oven for a few more minutes to set the white. This will stop the pastry going soggy when you put in the filling.

Next, make the filling. If it's baby spinach, don't chop it; if it's grown-up spinach, remove coarse stems and chop it roughly. Wash it thoroughly, place in a saucepan with a lid (don't add any extra water), and steam the spinach for 5 minutes – it wants to be thoroughly cooked. When it's steamed, press into the steamer to extract as much liquid as humanly possible. Pour away the excess liquid or keep for stock.

Beat the soft cheese into the two remaining eggs and the yolk from the third one. Add salt, pepper, nutmeg, the well-drained spinach and half the hard cheese. Pour the mixture into the pastry case. Scatter the remaining hard cheese over the top. Bake for 30 minutes or until set. Totally delicious.

SERVES 4 GENEROUSLY

The shortcrust pastry:

100g (4oz) wholemeal flour

100g (4oz) white flour

Pinch of salt

100g (4oz) unsalted butter

The filling:

3 eggs

350g (12oz) fresh spinach (baby spinach is best)

225g (8oz) cream cheese, ricotta, curd cheese or fromage frais

Salt and freshly ground black pepper

¼ tsp grated nutmeg

50g (2oz) Cheddar or Parmesan cheese, or a mixture

Potato and Kohlrabi Gratin

VEGETARIAN

Most people's reaction to receiving a kohlrabi from me is, "An alien jumped in the box!" Don't be scared of it, but don't fall in love with it as the Dutch have. Think of it as an eccentric friend: invite it around occasionally and enjoy it.

SERVES 6 AS A SIDE DISH

2 kohlrabi, peeled

2 medium main crop potatoes, peeled

Sea salt and freshly ground black pepper

2–3 handfuls of grated extra-sharp English Cheddar

½ mug of double cream

½ mug of milk

1 clove of garlic, peeled and finely chopped

Grated nutmeg

Start by slicing the kohlrabi and potatoes. If you have a mandolin (not the stringed instrument, although it would be nice to have some background music while you're cooking), slice both vegetables on a thin setting. If you haven't got one, slice a small cheek off each vegetable and sit them flat side down on your chopping board before slicing thinly – this will stop them rolling all over the place while you're trying to slice the veg and not your fingers.

In a butter-rubbed ceramic baking dish, layer alternately the kohl, spud, seasoning, cheese, kohl, spud, seasoning and cheese, finishing with a cheese layer.

Mix together the cream, milk and garlic and pour over the layered dish. Grate over some nutmeg. Bake on the middle shelf of the oven at 190°C/375°C/gas 5 for about 1–1½ hours. If the top starts to brown before the veg are cooked, pop a loose sheet of foil over the top and turn the oven down a touch.

Red Cabbage Braised in Balsamic Vinegar

VEGAN

Red cabbage holds my award for the most badly cooked vegetable in the UK. It can be delicious and if you don't think so, try this recipe. Red cabbage contains a lot of vitamin C, but this starts to break down once the cabbage has been cut so you should try to use it up within a few days. This means cabbage is ideal to use when you're entertaining – there'll be lots of it! Alternatively, you can keep the cooked dish in the fridge for a few days and simply warm and serve as you need it, but do not keep reheating from the same dish, just take out what you need. You can freeze it too.

Serve as a side dish with a roast, with a chop, with a sausage, with anything.

SERVES LOTS!

1 whole red cabbage

1 glug of olive oil

½ mug of balsamic vinegar

½ mug of sugar

Water

Salt and freshly ground black pepper (optional)

Wash the cabbage – you can use all the leaves, even the outer ones, in this recipe. Cut the cabbage in half through the centre core. Lay each half flat side down on a chopping board and shred the cabbage, discarding the white core.

Put the shredded cabbage into a heavy-based pot over a low heat with the oil, vinegar, sugar and half a cup of water and simmer with the lid on. Cook over a very low heat for about 1 hour, stirring every 10 minutes or so, adding a little water if necessary to make sure it doesn't dry out on the bottom of the pot. The cabbage is ready when it releases its natural sugars and is nice and tender. Season to taste.

Roasted Squash
and Wild Rocket Risotto

VEGETARIAN

When I was thinking about writing this book, the really clever publishing people came down to join me for lunch and I cooked this. Well, guess what? They decided to print the book, so go impress your friends and family with this recipe.

Don't be afraid to use pumpkin instead of squash or to add mushrooms and other types of greens like spinach or chard leaves.

Toss the diced squash in a little olive oil, season well with salt and pepper and place on a baking tray. Pop into a 190°C/375°F/gas 5 oven for 20 minutes or so, turning occasionally. Remove from the oven just when the outer edges start to brown off. Set aside to cool down and keep your picking fingers away from them, otherwise you won't have any to put into the risotto.

While they are cooling, sauté the onion with a glug of olive oil in a large heavy-based pot over a medium heat for 3–5 minutes. Add the rice and wine and slowly simmer until the wine has almost evaporated, stirring constantly. Now you start adding the stock to the rice a little at a time – as with the wine, you need to stir constantly and only add stock when the rice starts to thicken and get sticky. Keep the stock simmering in a separate saucepan. Continue doing this until the rice is cooked through and your arm is about to fall off.

Finally, when the rice is cooked through, add the cream and half the Parmesan, stir through the rocket and baked squash, season and remove from the heat when the risotto is nice and sticky. Sprinkle the remaining Parmesan over each dish and serve.

SERVES 4 AS A STARTER, OR 2 GENEROUSLY AS A MAIN COURSE

2 mugs of butternut squash, peeled and diced into 1cm (½in) cubes

Olive oil

Salt and freshly ground black pepper

1 onion, peeled and chopped

1 mug of risotto rice

½ mug of white wine

4 mugs of simmering chicken or vegetable stock

2 tbsp double cream

⅓ mug of grated Parmesan cheese

A couple handfuls of rocket leaves, chopped

Swede Chips with a Mug of Mustard Mayo

VEGETARIAN

This is just the thing to use up the most plentiful yet most vilified vegetable in Britain, and kids will love it!

You can keep this mayo in the fridge for a few days if there is any left over. Dollop some on a sandwich or a burger if you fancy. You can also thin it down with some olive oil and use it as a dressing.

Peel and trim the swede. Cut into chip-sized pieces about 1cm (½in) thick and place them in a bowl of water.

Heat the oil in a deep fryer or large saucepan to 160°C (320°F). Drain and dry the swede chips thoroughly and fry them in batches for about 3 minutes or until they float to the top and are tender but not crisp. Let these drain on kitchen paper and cool for 10–15 minutes.

Meanwhile, make the mayo. Place all the ingredients in a bowl and give them a good whisk. Season as desired and transfer to a mug.

Now heat the oil to 190°C (374°F) and refry the chips for another 3–4 minutes, until they are crisp and golden. Drain them on kitchen paper, season them with a little sea salt and serve straight away with your mug of mayo.

1 swede

Vegetable oil

The mayo:

⅓ mug of whole-egg mayonnaise (see page 84)

4 tbsp Dijon mustard

⅓ mug of natural yogurt

Juice of ½ a lemon

2 tsp freshly grated horseradish (optional)

2 or 3 grinds of sea salt

Balsamic Carrot Salad

VEGAN

This classic and simple salad goes wonderfully with roasts. It only works with fresh, organic carrots (conventionally farmed ones just won't be delicious enough).

SERVES 4

3–5 mugs of grated carrot (about 3–5 carrots)

A splash of balsamic vinegar

A splash of olive oil

1 small handful of toasted sliced almonds

1 small handful of raisins

Put the grated carrots in a salad bowl and add the balsamic vinegar and olive oil. You'll want the sweet flavour of the carrots to stand out, so take care not to add more than a splash of vinegar. Sprinkle the almonds on top and, finally, sprinkle the raisins over them. Serve at room temperature.

Fennel, Blood Orange
and Parmesan Salad

VEGETARIAN

This salad is tart and sweet and just great. It's something a bit different to make with blood oranges if you're orange-juiced-out. Preparing the oranges takes a bit of time, but if you're in a good mood you can meditate on their beautiful colour, and if you're in a bad mood you can relish pulling the fruit to bits. The salad goes especially well with fish and chicken, as well as with light pasta or rice dishes. You can also bulk it out by mixing in some green salad and/or home-made croûtons.

Remove any tough stalks from the fennel. Finely chop a few of the feathery leaves and reserve. Thinly slice the fennel and spread it out on a large plate. Now cut the blood orange into segments, and remove all the membranes. Spread the segments evenly over the fennel.

Drizzle the lemon juice on top, then lightly drizzle on some olive oil. Top it all off with some shaved Parmesan and the chopped fennel leaves.

SERVES 4

1 bulb fennel

2 blood oranges, peeled, pith removed

Juice of ½ lemon

Olive oil

2 handfuls of shaved Parmesan cheese

Custardy Pumpkin Pie

VEGETARIAN

I spent many years wondering why on earth Americans love pumpkin pie. Then I tried this one and the whole thing made sense – most of them aren't as lovely as this, but presumably everyone's eaten something this good once, and goes on dreaming of it for the rest of their days. Pumpkin pie makes a fair bit of sense – the flesh is very sweet and rich, and obviously those are good qualities for a pie. This pie is great hot or cold.

SERVES 6 8

½ small pumpkin, seeded (about 500g/1lb)

½ mug of sugar, or to taste

1 tbsp cornflour

½ tsp ground cinnamon

¼ tsp ground ginger

3 eggs, separated

1 tsp vanilla essence

310ml (10½fl oz) milk

½ teaspoon ground nutmeg

The pastry:

A pinch of salt

210g (7½oz) flour

100g (4oz) cold butter

3–4 tbsp cold water

To serve:

whipped cream, double cream or ice cream

crystallised ginger

If you're feeling lazy or just don't want to make a pie base, skip the pastry bit, make the custard mixture, pour it into a buttered baking dish and cook as if it were the pie.

Preheat the oven to 190°C/375°F/gas 5. Cut the pumpkin in half and scoop out the seeds. Put a piece of aluminium foil on a baking sheet or in a large baking tin and pop the pumpkin onto it, cut side down. Cover well with more foil. Bake for about 1 hour or until the pumpkin is tender. While it's baking, make your pie base.

To make your pastry, first mix the salt into the flour. Add the cold butter and cut it into the flour with two knives or give it a few blasts in a food processor. Slowly sprinkle in the cold water until the pastry just holds together. Take care not to handle the pastry too much or to over-process it. Pop the dough in a bag in the fridge for at least half an hour.

Roll out the dough on a floured surface and lift into a greased pie pan. Crimp the edges and prick the base all over with a fork, then pop into the bottom of the oven for 5–10 minutes. This should help your pastry stay crisp when you pour in the filling. If you want super-crunch for your pastry, brush some milk or egg white onto the pastry a couple of minutes before you take it out of the oven at this stage.

When the pumpkin is soft, hoik it out of the oven and let it cool a bit. Spoon out the pumpkin flesh and purée it in a food processor or press through a strainer, discarding the skin. Show the pumpkin no mercy at this stage – it must be super smooth! Weigh out 250ml (8fl oz) of the purée for this recipe and freeze any extra. (Pumpkin purée keeps nicely in the freezer, so you can simply defrost any extra when you feel like another pie, or throw it into bread or muffins when you are baking.)

Once the purée has cooled, stir in the sugar, cornflour, cinnamon and ginger. Then mix in the egg yolks, vanilla essence and milk. In a separate bowl, beat the egg whites until frothy, but not stiff. Gently fold into the pumpkin mixture. Pour into the pie base and sprinkle the nutmeg on top.

Bake at 210°C/410F/gas 6½ for 10 minutes, then lower the heat to 180°C/350°F/gas 4 and bake for a further 30 minutes, or until set in the middle and lightly browned at the edges. Serve with fresh whipped cream, double cream or ice cream and a few chunks of crystallized ginger.

Leek, Potato and Spinach Frittata

VEGETARIAN

So simple, so tasty, so Spanish, so have you got a spare 20 minutes?

**SERVES 4 AS A
LIGHT MEAL**

1 large or 2 medium main
crop potatoes, peeled

A few glugs of olive oil

1 leek (tough dark green
top removed)

1 red onion, peeled and
finely diced

3 good handfuls of
spinach (or chard),
chopped

4 large eggs, lightly
beaten and seasoned

2 handfuls of grated
cheese, such as Cheddar

Pinch of paprika

Salt and freshly ground
black pepper

First things first, preheat the oven to 190°C/375°F/gas 5.

Dice the potato into 1cm (½in) pieces and pop them into a medium to
hot ovenproof frying pan with a few glugs of olive oil. Give them a toss
every minute or so while cooking.

While they are sizzling away, wash and chop your leek by splitting it
lengthways from the root end three or four times (don't cut through
the root or the layers will come apart). Rinse the leek and then chop
into finger-width pieces – the root has served its purpose now so you
can chop it off and bin it!

When the potatoes are golden brown and cooked through, throw in
your leek and onion and give these a toss. Keep moving them around
until the onion becomes softened and translucent. Turn the heat down
to low and spread the spinach on top of the other veg, lightly pressing
down with the back of a spatula for another minute or so until the
spinach starts to wilt.

Now pour over your eggs and top with cheese. Sprinkle with paprika
and seasoning and put into the oven for about 10–12 minutes or until
the top is nice and golden. Remove from the oven and let it sit for 2
minutes before slicing and serving.

Spinach and Yogurt Purée

VEGETARIAN

This is a simple all-rounder that can be put together in minutes and used with all kinds of dishes, such as grilled lamb or chicken or rice, or even served as a dip.

A slightly chunkier sauce is another very nice alternative: instead of puréeing the ingredients together, finely chop the spinach and just mix all the ingredients.

Remove the spinach stalks and wash the leaves. Roughly chop the leaves, toss into a saucepan with a lid and steam for about 5–6 minutes. Squeeze out any excess water and purée in a food processor with the garlic, lemon juice and yogurt until it's nice and smooth. Season to taste and serve.

MAKES 2 MUGS

Spinach – about a handful when held by the stalks

1–2 garlic cloves, peeled and crushed

A squeeze of fresh lemon juice

1 mug of natural yogurt

Salt and freshly ground black pepper

Roasted Garlic and Apple Chutney

VEGAN

This is a great chutney to make at the start of the apple season, so it has enough time to settle before the Christmas cheese overload begins.

MAKES ABOUT 7 GOOD-SIZED JAM JARS

1 whole bulb of garlic

3 large onions, peeled and chopped into small chunks

1.5kg (3lb) apples, cored and roughly chopped into small chunks

A good couple of handfuls of sultanas or raisins

1 tsp ground coriander

1 tsp paprika

1 tsp Chinese five spice powder or mixed spice (or make your own with a pinch of ginger and one of cinnamon) or just throw in a cinnamon stick

1 tsp salt

1 mug of brown sugar (white will also do)

2 mugs of malt vinegar

Preheat the oven to 190°C/375°F/gas 5.

The first thing to do is slice the very top off the garlic bulb so that you can just see the flesh of the garlic cloves through the skin. Pop this onto a baking tray, top side up, and into a medium-hot oven. The garlic should take about 45 minutes to roast, so start preparing and cooking the other ingredients meanwhile.

Put all the other ingredients into a large saucepan and bring to the boil. Give them a stir now and then and bring back to a simmer. When your garlic is roasted (it'll be soft and squishy), squeeze the garlic from the root end out of the bulb and into the pot. Let the chutney simmer uncovered for about 1½–2 hours, stirring every now and then. Feel free to add a little more sugar or vinegar to the pot to get your chutney the way you like it.

The chutney should be ready when it becomes a thick porridge-like consistency. Spoon this into sterilised jars, close, cool and store in the cupboard until Christmas.

Mulled Wine, Pears and Clementines with Dark Chocolate Shavings

VEGETARIAN

I got this one from Gary, who I've worked with for years. Like Gary, it's a very laid back dish and not a lot can go wrong with it.

SERVES 6

6 large, firm pears such as Conference, Comice and Concord (which is a hybrid of Conference and Comice) – Williams will work fine too

1 orange

4 cloves

½ mug of brown sugar

1 cinnamon stick

1cm (½in) of ginger, grated

A really good grating of nutmeg

1½ mugs of red wine

3 clementines, peeled and segmented, leaving the pith on

Crème fraîche (optional – a few spoonfuls stirred into the finished syrup make it a bit less intense)

To serve:

Vanilla ice cream

Dark chocolate

Use a lidded saucepan that's deep enough for the pears to stand up in, and will hold them quite closely together. Peel the pears and take a thin slice off the bottom so they will stand upright. Leave the stalks on for easy handling. Place them in the pan.

Cut the orange in half, squeeze the juice into the pot and cut off a 2.5cm (1in) strip of orange peel. Stud this with the cloves and add it to the pan.

Put the sugar and spices in the pan, then pour in the wine (add enough to just cover the pears). Simmer this with the lid on for about 35 minutes, then add the clementine segments and simmer for a further 10 minutes, so the pears are nice and tender.

When the pears are done, remove them from the pot by the stalk and place on individual dessert plates or bowls. Remove the clementine segments and divide these between the plates.

Now remove the slice of orange peel and cinnamon stick from the pot and crank up the heat so the cooking liquid reduces to a syrup – this will take about 7–10 minutes. Stir in the crème fraîche if using it. Drizzle the hot syrup over the pears and serve with a good scoop of vanilla ice cream with shavings of dark chocolate over the top.

Autumn Assortment

For the days when your fridge is a little bare, or you just don't feel like following a recipe but you do feel like treating your body to some good stuff, here are a few easy autumnal treats to use up your spare fruit and vegetables.

Fruit compote

Cause for celebration when you find squidgy apples or pears at the bottom of your fruit bowl! Quantities really don't matter with this – you can use one piece of fruit or the whole bowlful, and you can add extra ingredients at the end to tweak the flavour.

- Cut up the apples and/or pears and core them. For mega-mush, peel them too

- Melt some butter in a pan

- Fry the apples along with some cinnamon (essential!) and a bit of sugar if the apples aren't super-sweet

- You can also add some powdered ginger or a vanilla pod if you like; or lemon zest, lemon juice or some raisins. You could probably put a sheep in there and it would still taste nice

- Add a little water to the pan

- Then you just cook it, stirring occasionally, until it looks good

- After about 30 minutes you will have a sublimely delicious mush which is great with yogurt or cream or granola or just as it is, hot or cold

Preserves

Autumn is a good time of year to make chutneys and things like onion marmalade. The best chutneys I've ever eaten were made by John the Builder, a legendary figure in Abel & Cole's history. John virtually lived in our warehouse for years, building new things for us and mending the things we'd broken (or those that he had – I was never sure). In his spare time, John used to cook up the veggies we had left over or tried to throw away, making vast buckets (literally) of knockout chutneys. Unfortunately, John could never remember what he put in them, and I will therefore have to suggest that you check out Delia or some other authority on this one. Or you could give John a call . . .

Autumn Juices

If you're getting out the juicer, I'm sure you don't need me to tell you that it's a good idea to put every reasonable vegetable you can find through it before you tackle the washing up. Have some fun and see what works. If you are following these recipes carefully, though, my quantities are enough for two people.

Cold or Hot Sweet Orchard A.P.L.

This has a little zing and zang about it. It's the kind of juice you could put a shot of dark rum into for a little extra kick! Or leave out the lime (you can keep the rum!), add a cinnamon stick instead, and warm it up for a lovely, cosy autumnal drink.

3 apples | 2 pears | ½ lime, rind included – just push the whole thing through the juicer

Captain Cucarrot

Light and refreshing. Another one for the juicer:

½ cucumber | 4 carrots | A small knob of ginger

Michele's Magic

This was invented by Michele Simeon, beloved Abel & Cole staff member, who was whisked off to Finland by her prince charming. Thank goodness she left us this recipe to toast her health!

Put through the juicer:

2 apples | 1 stick celery | as much ginger as you can take | a shot of Finnish vodka if nobody's looking . . .

Gone with the Wind

Juicetastic!

3 carrots | 1 stick of celery | 1 kohlrabi or cabbage leaves | Handful of parsley

And if it's too late for any of that . . .

. . . why not invest in some wriggly worms? They live in a specially designed worm colony which is capable of demolishing scraps in no time. My wriggly worms are without doubt the hardest-working members of my family, and I know them each by name. You can also transfer a delegation of worms into your compost bin to keep things moving as the weather gets colder.

Winter

With the trees going bald and the journeys both to and from work in the dark, I think it's helpful to remind yourself of two things: the sun always shines in space and half the fun of a good summer holiday is the food. To banish those winter blues:

Do . . .

- Book a holiday for some time in the New Year: this needn't be to a top-ten global holiday destination – a trip to see a great friend at the other end of the county will do the trick.

- Get creative in the kitchen, with creative being the operative word. That's why the recipes I've included here allow for plenty of variation and creativity from you. And don't forget the first rule of cooking in winter: you must be playing music so start by plugging your iPod into the toaster.

Don't . . .

- Look out of the window.

- Watch too much reality TV. They never show you the bits where the participants are bored stupid.

- Look in the mirror: save that until around March.

A great thing to eat this time of year is game. Some people feel it's a little unnecessary to actually shoot what you eat, given the fact that more "humane" modern methods of extracting meat from animals exist. Having spent my fair share of time both wandering through abattoirs and wandering around farms that offer shoots, I'd like to give you my thoughts on wild vs free-range meat.

If I had the choice of being a chicken or a pheasant, I know what I would rather be. It's a no brainer (and I don't mean the chicken). Comparing free-range (even organic free-range) and wild is like comparing permission for a sleepover with an all-night rave. The very best organic chicken at 16 weeks trumps the inorganic "£1.99 special" by about 10 weeks. However, even your least lucky pheasant who succumbs to the road at the start of the season will have reached "organic" age, and by the end of the season the Irish pheasant will have matured to a full six months.

Happily, vegetables attract no such journey into the moral maze. Admittedly, winter is a tricky time to be eating local vegetables, but crack it and you'll be surprised at how good it makes you feel. It's not that there's anything criminal about the green beans grown under street lights and flown in from Kenya; just as there's nothing illegal about the 4-by-4 that does the school run in town or about the bottled mineral water I saw a woman pouring into her windscreen washer reservoir the other day (much as I wish there were). But I always get a much more satisfying feeling out of making a delicious meal from things grown just up the road.

The local vegetables we eat in the winter are all those that have traditionally been cooked rather blandly and are often described as "staples". The truth of it is that they are the plants that were great at hibernating underground over the winter months, thereby providing our ancestors with nutrition all the way through until springtime and beyond.

I think we have two problems with these vegetables: first, they are considered old-fashioned, and secondly the recipes for them have been put together rather prescriptively, rather like cooking by numbers and not allowing much room for creative flair.

You're never going to make a masterpiece by joining the dots, so use these recipes as guidelines from which to get creative. This will also make the whole process of cooking much less stressful. Don't you just hate it when you read the ingredients for a recipe that you want to knock together of a Tuesday evening and it says things like "and most crucially, add some cold-sour fat gherkins", as if the whole dish would be a disaster if you didn't make a detour via Liechtenstein on the way back from work?

In short, mingle with Mozart, remember mustard powder is a great substitute for most exotic spices, and if you fancy beetroot but haven't got any, substitute parsnips and red cabbage. And if you're missing even them in the bottom of your vegetable drawer, you need to get those organic delivery people in your life!

Winter is the season for . . .

parsnips • swede • turnips • leeks • cauliflower • cabbages • celeriac • kale • chicory • Jerusalem artichokes • Sicilian blood oranges

Caramelised Shallot Croûtons

VEGETARIAN

Snazzy onions on toast! Some of the simplest things in life are often the best. Serve these with a soup or as a light snack. They make a great rustic hors d'oeuvres.

SERVES 6

12 x 1cm (½in) slices of baguette, cut on the angle

6 shallots, peeled and sliced

4 sprigs of thyme, stalk removed

A good glug of olive oil

Salt to taste

Freshly grated Romano or Parmesan cheese

Preheat the oven to 190°C/375°F/gas 5.

Place the bread on a baking tray and bake for about 5 minutes or until lightly toasted, then remove from the oven.

Sauté the shallots and thyme in olive oil over a medium heat for about 7–8 minutes until the shallots are golden brown and caramelised. Season with salt and take off the heat.

Top the croûtons with the shallots, sprinkle with the cheese and bake or grill until the tops are brown.

Bacon and Eggs
with Apple and Parsnip

This makes a perfect brunch. Serve with wholemeal toast.

SERVES 4

6 rashers of back bacon, diced

Knob of butter

1 onion, peeled and diced

3 medium parsnips, peeled and diced

1 red pepper, diced

1 large or 2 small apples (any variety), peeled, cored and diced

4 large eggs

Sea salt and freshly ground black pepper

A couple of good pinches of chopped fresh thyme

Fry the bacon in a large frying pan over a medium heat until crispy. Remove with a slotted spoon and drain on kitchen paper. Drain most of the fat from the pan.

Now add the knob of butter and onion to the same pan and sauté for a few minutes before adding the parsnips. Cook this for about 10 minutes and be sure to keep the parsnips moving in the pan until they become golden in colour. Throw in the red pepper and apple, put the bacon back into the pan and give it a good toss around for about a further 3 minutes.

Meanwhile, poach or fry the eggs, keeping the yolks runny.

Season the apple and parsnip mixture with salt and pepper, stir through the thyme and serve with a runny egg on top.

Easy Peasy Halibut Chowder

It's easy, it's peas-y, using frozen is fine.
Great with fresh crusty bread and a nice glass of wine.

SERVES 6

4 rashers streaky bacon, diced

A glug of olive oil

1 large onion, peeled and chopped

4 mugs of fish stock (veg stock works nicely too)

4 potatoes, peeled and diced

1 stalk of celery, diced

500g (1lb) halibut (or any other firm white fish), cut into 2.5cm (1in) cubes

½ mug of peas (frozen ones are fine)

2 tbsp flour

½ tsp sugar

3 tbsp water

½ mug of milk

½ mug of single cream

Salt and freshly ground black pepper

Small bunch of chopped parsley

Fry the bacon until crisp in a glug of olive oil in a large pan, then add the onion and cook until translucent. Add the stock, spuds and celery and simmer for about 15 minutes, then add the fish and peas. Allow to simmer gently for a further 5 minutes.

Mix the flour, sugar and water together until completely smooth and add this to the pot, stirring continuously for another minute or so. Then add the milk and cream and simmer for a further 5 minutes. Season with salt and serve in warm bowls. Garnish with the parsley and finish with a few grinds of pepper.

Scotch Broth

This is the kind of winter dish that makes you enjoy the British (or Scottish, even) climate . . . and that's saying something. It's not a glamorous dish but you just have to cook it once a year. Only buy the mutton when the forecast is for freezing temps and it's February. Remember to start this recipe the night before as the dried peas need soaking. Adding the roux makes for a thicker broth.

Put the mutton neck, barley, peas and a little seasoning into a large pan with the water. Bring to the boil, then reduce to a simmer for about an hour with the lid on.

Add the celery, carrot, leek, onion and turnip and continue simmering for 30 minutes, then add the cabbage and simmer for a further 15 minutes.

In a small separate pot over a medium-low heat, start making your roux by melting the butter and stirring in the flour with a wooden spoon for about 5 minutes, until you have a very smooth paste. Put this to one side.

Now remove the mutton neck from the large pot. Cut the meat from the bones and return the meat to the broth. Skim off any fat from the broth and stir through your roux to thicken. Season, throw in the parsley and serve in warm bowls with lots of crusty bread on the side.

SERVES ABOUT 4

About 500g (1lb) of mutton neck, trimmed of excess fat

⅓ mug of pearl barley

½ mug of dried peas, soaked overnight and then rinsed

Salt and freshly ground black pepper

6 mugs of water

1 stick of celery, sliced

1 large carrot, sliced

1 small leek, sliced

1 large onion, peeled and diced

1 small turnip, peeled and diced

About two handfuls of shredded cabbage

A small handful of chopped parsley

The roux:

2 tbsp butter

2 tbsp flour

Vanilla-Roasted Loin of Pork

SERVES 6

1kg (2¼lb) pork loin, boned and trimmed of fat

2 vanilla pods

A couple of sprigs of fresh thyme leaves

Salt and freshly ground pepper

A glug of olive oil

The brine:

3 mugs of cold water

½ mug of salt

½ mug of sugar

2 vanilla pods, split and seeds scraped (use both pod and seeds in the brine)

A splash of vanilla essence (optional)

A couple of bay leaves

A couple of sprigs of parsley

1 tsp peppercorns

Salt and pepper

This recipe comes from my old friend Gary. One evening, we took some old withered beetroot out of the vegetable basket and stuck them in the hot bit of the Aga without even washing them, before we kicked off with the rest of the cooking. The beetroot cooked in the oven for about 1½ hours. With about 25 minutes to go until the beetroot and pork were ready, we split some fennel and threw it in with the pork. Gary put the trim of the pork in the back of the oven for Deputy Dog, who'd been away at dog school all week, and we served it all up with steamed kale, burgundy and a great CD that my sister made for me. Repeat for a completely perfect evening.

Serve with Braised Red Cabbage (see page 144) or the Parsnip and Shallot Thingamabob (see page 193).

Start by making your brine in a glass or plastic dish (not metal or aluminium). Just mix up all the ingredients until all the sugar and salt have dissolved. Submerge the pork in the brine and leave it to soak for about 2–3 hours in the refrigerator.

Preheat the oven to 190°C/375°F/gas 5.

Remove the pork from the brine and dry with a tea towel – Gary prefers to use a newspaper, but that's just him. Split a couple more vanilla pods and scrape out the seeds. Rub the pork loin all over with the vanilla seeds, sprinkle the thyme leaves on the inside of the loin and tie up with butchers' string, leaving the empty vanilla pods inside the pork with the thyme. Then give it a grind of salt and pepper over the top.

Pour a glug of olive oil into a very hot ovenproof pan and sear the pork loin to a golden colour on all sides. Transfer the pan to the oven for about 30–40 minutes until done. Let the pork rest for a good 10 minutes before carving.

Venison Saltimbocca

Lots of deer get run over near where I live. My landlord dropped over some wild Hampshire roadkill once and we cooked it this way. Huge success. The Italians love this dish with pasta.

The first thing you need to do is flatten the venison steaks with a meat hammer or a wooden rolling pin. Do this between two pieces of cling film and flatten them until they have doubled in size and are about 1cm (½in) thick.

Now lay two slices of the ham on each venison steak, followed by a slice of mozzarella and finished with a sage leaf and seasoning to taste. Roll up the steaks, tucking in the ends and stitching with a couple of wooden toothpicks. Finish by dusting them lightly with flour. These little bundles are your saltimbocca.

Melt a knob of butter in a frying pan over a medium heat and sauté the saltimbocca until lightly browned and cooked through. Next, add a couple of glugs of Marsala or sherry and flame the pan (you can use a match to do this or the flame from the hob). When the flames go out, add a good knob of butter and toss the saltimbocca around. Garnish with the parsley and serve with a wild winter salad.

SERVES 4 AS A STARTER

4 venison sirloin steaks

8 slices of prosciutto ham

4 slices of mozzarella

4 large sage leaves

Salt and freshly ground black pepper

A light dusting of flour

2 large knobs of butter

A couple of good glugs of Marsala or sweet sherry

A couple of pinches of chopped parsley for garnish

Venison Fillet with Black Kale and Port, Stilton and Olive Sauce

This is the kind of dish Nelson would have eaten on 20 October 1805 (don't you just love Google!). Rich, unusual, a real effort and well worth it. If the boss is coming over for dinner try this . . . and don't skimp on the wine. A gutsy Tempranillo or something Pinot Noir-based will do the job very nicely.

Heat a knob of butter in a heavy-based saucepan over a medium heat and sauté the shallots or onions for a couple of minutes. Add the port and stock, bring it to the boil and then turn down to a simmer for about 20 minutes or until it has reduced by about half the amount.

Preheat the oven to 200°C/400°F/gas 6.

While the sauce is reducing, heat a little oil in a very hot pan and sear the venison fillets on all sides to give them some good colour, then transfer to an ovenproof dish. Cook for about 5–10 minutes in the oven until medium rare (depends on the size of the fillets; over-cooking will make them tough). Remove from the oven and let them rest on a warm plate for 5–10 minutes – the longer the better.

While the venison is resting, steam or boil the kale for 5 minutes until tender, drain it and put it back into the pot. Stir through the butter and give it a good seasoning before piling in stacks on warm plates.

Drain any juice from the resting venison into the sauce. Remove from the heat, add the Stilton, olives and thyme and stir through. Slice the venison fillets into finger-width coins and plate up over the kale. Spoon the sauce over and serve.

SERVES 4

A knob of butter for the sauce and a couple of knobs for the kale

⅓ mug of shallots, peeled and thinly sliced, or onion, peeled and chopped

½ mug of port

1 mug of beef stock

Glug of olive oil

Enough venison fillet for 4 people

A bag of black kale, or any other variety will do, washed and chopped

Salt and freshly ground black pepper

½–¾ mug of crumbled Stilton – add more or less to your liking

⅓ mug of pitted black olives, chopped

1 tbsp fresh, chopped thyme

Not Another Duck and Orange Recipe!

The reason there are a lot of duck and orange recipes is that they go together like egg and chips. I think ducks must have originally been eaten in orange groves although I've not heard any quacking in Sicily. This dish is rich. Make sure you've got the Rennies to hand.

You'll need to start this dish in the morning, as it's best when left to marinate.

SERVES 4

2 duck breasts with the skin left on

½ mug freshly squeezed orange juice for the marinade

¼ mug light soy sauce

2 glugs of vegetable oil of your choice

2 tbsp honey

1 tbsp white wine vinegar

A few good gratings of orange zest

1 tsp paprika

A good pinch of sea salt

Start by scoring the skin of the breasts diagonally both ways so you have a small diamond pattern all over them. Whisk together all the remaining ingredients in a glass bowl, add the duck, cover and refrigerate for about 8 hours or more, turning occasionally.

Remove the duck from the bowl (keep the marinade) and pat dry with kitchen paper.

Heat up a heavy-based frying pan, add the duck breasts skin side down and sear for about 5 minutes to get some good colour developing on the skin. Drain off the fat, reduce the heat to medium and cook for a further 10 minutes or so (reduce the heat further if the skin starts to burn). Drain the fat again, turn the breast over and cook on a low heat for about 10 minutes or until cooked to your liking. Remove the duck to a warm plate to rest while you make the sauce.

Drain the remaining fat from the pan, put it back onto a medium heat and deglaze with a wooden spoon and a little water. Add the marinade to the pan and bring to the boil, then bring it back to a good strong simmer to reduce and thicken for about 5 minutes or so.

When the sauce has reduced, slice the breasts across the grain into 1cm (½in) thick slices and put onto four warm plates. Add any juice from the duck breasts to the sauce and strain through a sieve before serving with the duck.

Game Bird in a Loaf Tin

The big problem with pheasant and partridge is that they have a tendency to dry out. Not cooked this way, they don't! This is good with the Celeriac and Mascarpone Purée on page 199.

SERVES 2

1 pheasant or partridge

Sea salt and freshly ground black pepper

1 leek, washed and chopped into 2.5cm (1in) pieces

2 bay leaves

A couple of sprigs of thyme

A couple of sprigs of rosemary

1 mug of chicken stock (approximately)

1 mug of red wine (approximately)

Preheat the oven to 190°C/375°F/gas 5.

Season the inside and outside of the bird well and stuff with the chopped leek. Place the bay leaves, thyme and rosemary into the bottom of an 800g (2lb) loaf tin. Then put in the bird, breast side down so it's a nice tight fit. Slowly pour in equal parts wine and stock so it comes halfway up the bird.

Cover the top of the loaf tin with foil and bake for about 30 minutes before removing the foil and baking for a further 15 to 20 minutes or until cooked. Drain the juices from the tin onto a warm serving dish and then turn the bird out on top.

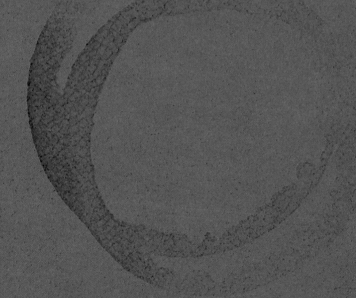

The One and Only Traditional Cornish Pasty!

These are great to make with the kids – they can make their own pasty and label them by placing a pastry shape on top. These quantities should make around four large pasties; just multiply the pastry and other ingredients for more. Our guess is you will probably need it!

Start off by making the pastry. Rub the butter and lard into the flour and salt – don't be too heavy-handed – until it's like breadcrumbs (this can be done with a couple of blasts in a food processor). Then add cold water and stir in with a fork until it holds together to make a dough. If you're doing this last stage in the food processor, be careful not to over-process it. Rest the dough for 20 minutes before you roll it out.

While the pastry is resting, finely slice the steak. Slice the potato and turnip or swede into smallish thin pieces and throw these all in a bowl with the diced onion and sliced steak. Mix and season well with salt and pepper.

Using a floured tabletop, roll out a quarter of the pastry to a circle the size of a dinner plate. Make a mound of a quarter of the filling just off centre on the pastry. Dampen round the edge of the pastry with either water or milk. Fold the pastry over to make a half-moon shape, crimping the edges with your fingers. Make a small slit on top to let out steam and brush with beaten egg to glaze. Repeat with the remaining pastry and filling. Chill for half an hour before you cook it.

Preheat the oven to 190°C/375°F/gas 5.

Place the pasties on a lightly greased metal baking tray and slide into the middle of the oven. Cook for about 40 minutes. The pasties are cooked when their undersides turn brown and crisp. Let them cool for a few minutes before eating.

MAKES 4

Pastry (sorry, folks, you will need some scales for this):

125g (4½oz) cold butter, cubed

125g (4½oz) lard

500g (1lb) plain flour

A good pinch of salt

2–3 tbsp cold water

beaten egg, to glaze

Splash of water or milk

Beaten egg, to glaze

Filling:

500g (1lb) organic steak (use chuck or skirt)

Two large potatoes, peeled

½ large turnip or swede, peeled

1 large onion, peeled and diced

Salt and lots of freshly ground black pepper

Cauliflower Winter Curry

VEGETARIAN

SERVES 6–8

2 knobs of butter

2 garlic cloves, peeled and minced

5cm (2in) piece of ginger, grated

1–2 chillies, minced

2 tsp ground cumin

1 tsp ground coriander

1 tsp ground turmeric

2 tins tomatoes, chopped

1 mug of vegetable stock or water

1 tbsp tamarind concentrate (optional)

1 head cauliflower, cut into bite-size chunks

2 potatoes, peeled and cubed

1 parsnip, peeled and cubed

1 mug of cooked chickpeas (or a tin of them)

Juice of ½ lime

1 mug of natural yogurt

1 small bunch of fresh mint, chopped, or 2 tsp dried

1 small bunch of fresh coriander, chopped, or 2 tsp dried

Salt and freshly ground black pepper

This is a great winter curry that you can have fun experimenting with. The potatoes and parsnip can be exchanged for different root vegetables or squashes. Try throwing in some chard or other green leafy goodness a couple of minutes before the end. Like all curries, this is even better the day after you've cooked it – those who eat their leftover takeouts for breakfast the next day know what they're doing!

Melt the butter in a large pot over a medium heat and add the garlic, ginger and chillies. Sauté briefly, then add the cumin, coriander and turmeric, and give the mixture a couple of stirs. Add the tomatoes and stock to the pot and bring to a simmer. Dissolve the tamarind concentrate in a tablespoon or two of hot water and add to the pot. Next stir in the vegetables and chickpeas. Cover and simmer for 15 minutes, until the veggies are tender.

Remove from heat and stir in the lime, yogurt and fresh herbs. Season with salt and pepper to taste. Serve on a bed of basmati rice. Winter curry tastes delicious with chutney and toasted cashews on the side.

Seared Cornish Scallops
with Sticky Chicory

This is the sort of thing you'd expect a celebrity chef to knock together if you dropped in on them unannounced. It's one of those recipes where you get an enormous amount of flavour for every minute spent in the kitchen.

SERVES 4

1 onion, peeled and finely diced

1 garlic clove, peeled and thinly sliced

1 knob of butter

6 heads fresh chicory

Juice and zest of 1 orange

Juice and zest of 1 lemon

½ mug of white wine

½ mug of sugar

2 sprigs of fresh thyme, stalks removed

Salt and freshly ground black pepper

Olive oil

12 large scallops

Balsamic vinegar

Start by sautéing the onion and garlic in a good-sized frying pan with a knob of butter. While these are cooking, finely slice the chicory heads lengthways, discarding the base and core if any. Add these to the pan along with all of the orange and half the lemon juice, the zests, wine, sugar and thyme. Bring to the boil, then reduce to a simmer for about 10 minutes, or until the chicory starts to caramelise. Remove the pan from the heat and season to taste.

Heat a little olive oil in a very hot non-stick pan, season the scallops well and sear on one side for 1 minute. Turn them over and cook for a further minute, adding a squeeze of lemon juice just before taking them off the heat.

Put a good dollop of the chicory in the centre of each of four plates, and place the scallops around the edge. Drizzle around the plate with a little good-quality olive oil and balsamic vinegar.

Serve immediately. No ifs and buts. No, you can't watch the end of that programme.

Citrus Potato Cakes

VEGETARIAN

These go very well with pork or fish. They beat baked potatoes and are not much more difficult.

Start by rubbing the potatoes with olive oil and pricking them all over with a fork. Pop them on a tray and into a 190°C/375°F/gas 5 oven for about an hour, or until the skins are nice and crispy.

When the potatoes are done, slice them in half. Scoop all the flesh out into a bowl and let it cool for 10 minutes. Add the orange and lime zest, the nutmeg, a good pinch of salt, the cloves, orange juice and egg yolk. Mash this all together and then flatten out the mix onto a lightly floured cutting board.

Cut out eight 2.5cm (1in) thick patties with a pastry cutter, or shape them by hand. Lightly flour the tops of the cakes, then fry in butter for 3–5 minutes on each side until golden brown.

SERVES 4 AS A SIDE DISH

4 baking potatoes

A glug of olive oil

zest of ½ an orange

zest of ½ a lime

A good grating of nutmeg

Sea salt

A pinch of ground cloves

2 tsp orange juice

1 egg yolk

Flour, for dusting

Butter, for frying

Roasted Beetroot Penne

VEGETARIAN

Pasta might not be the obvious thing to cook when you want to impress your guests, but I promise that this recipe will bring forth a few gasps the first time you serve it – in a good way! Beetroot is sometimes mixed straight into raw pasta dough to give it extra colour and flavour, but beetroot as a pasta topping is far rarer than it should be. Roasting the beetroot allows it to retain its wonderfully earthy flavour. This dish goes really nicely with a rocket or mixed herb salad and a bottle of dry white wine.

SERVES 4

About 700g (1lb 6oz) beetroot

A few good glugs of olive oil

400g (14oz) penne or other chunky pasta

3 garlic cloves, peeled and minced

Juice of ½ lemon

½ mug of single cream

To garnish:

Plenty of freshly grated Parmesan cheese

Toasted walnuts, finely chopped

Chopped fresh parsley or basil (optional)

Preheat the oven to 190°C/375°F/gas 5. Place the whole beetroot in an oiled baking pan, rub with olive oil and cover tightly with foil. Roast the beetroot until fork tender. The cooking time will vary according to the size of the beetroot, but will probably be around 1–1 ½ hours.

When the beetroot is cooked through, remove it from the oven and set aside to cool. Meanwhile, start boiling a pan of water for the pasta and preparing the other ingredients. When the water has boiled, add the pasta and cook according to the packet instructions.

Now peel the beetroot (the skin should slip off easily), remove any remaining stems or hard bits, and cut into bite-sized chunks. Sauté the garlic in a pan with a few glugs of olive oil for a couple of minutes over a medium heat. Then add the beetroot and sauté for a further few minutes to ensure it's hot. Stir in the lemon juice and mix well. Lower the heat and gradually add the cream, cooking for about 2–3 minutes until just hot.

Spoon the creamy beetroot mixture over the drained pasta and top with lots of Parmesan, toasted walnuts and fresh herbs, if using.

If you have leftovers, try tossing them with a block of crumbled feta or goats' cheese and some olive oil and bake in a greased baking pan at medium heat for about 20 minutes, until heated throughout and slightly crunchy on top. You'll end up with a rather colourful and sophisticated version of macaroni cheese!

Tempura Sea Bass
on Celeriac Remoulade

SERVES 4

The remoulade:

About 500g (1lb) celeriac (weight before peeling)

1 red onion, peeled and thinly sliced

½ mug of mustard mayo – see page 84 or just mix 1–2 tsp mustard powder into 4 dsp of mayonnaise

Salt and freshly ground black pepper

Handful of chopped parsley

The tempura sea bass:

Salt and freshly ground black pepper

⅔ mug of plain flour

1 egg

⅔ mug of cold water with 1 ice cube in it

2 tbsp dry white wine

Sea bass fillets – about 1 fillet per person, skinned and sliced at an angle into 2.5 x 10cm (1 x 4in) chunks

500ml (17fl oz) groundnut oil, for frying

A little light soy sauce or sweet chilli sauce, to serve

Make sure to buy responsibly fished sea bass, so there's some left in the sea for your grandchildren. You can also cook this with any other white fish. Do yourself a favour and get the fishmonger to skin it for you! The trick to great tempura is the use of cold water – it stops the batter from getting too oily when frying.

First, make the remoulade. Peel the celeriac, then slice it as finely as possible (use a mandolin if you have one). Stack the slices a few at a time on top of each other and cut into long, thin julienne strips. Place in a bowl and mix with the sliced onion and mustard mayo. Check the seasoning and stir in the parsley.

To make the batter, mix some salt and pepper into the flour on a plate. In a large bowl, beat the egg and mix with the water and wine. Add the flour and whisk quickly until smooth. Use immediately. Dredge the fish in the seasoned flour before dipping in the batter.

Heat about 2.5cm (1in) of peanut oil in a deep-sided pot or wok to 185°C (365°F). If you don't have a thermometer, worry not. Put the heat up to the highest temperature, and once it is very hot, test a small piece of fish in the batter to see if it is right. In any case, it's not a bad idea to fry and try just one piece of fish first to get the timing right and make sure it's cooked properly before doing it in batches.

With some chopsticks (if you can!) or tongs (if you can't!), dip the fish pieces into the batter and slip them into the oil. Make sure you do this in small batches so that you don't lose the temperature of the oil. Fry these, turning occasionally, until the batter becomes a nice golden brown colour. Remove them with a slotted spoon and place on kitchen paper to drain a little. Keep warm while frying the remainder of the fish, then serve on top of the remoulade.

Parsnip and Shallot Thingamabob

VEGETARIAN

This dish has a wonderful sweet and sour thing going on and will go very nicely with a roast.

Sauté the shallots and parsnips with a glug of olive oil in a large frying pan over a medium heat for about 10 minutes or until they turn a nice golden brown colour.

Now add a good squeeze of honey to coat and add the wine. Continue to cook for 3–5 minutes until all the wine has disappeared, then add a few glugs of white wine vinegar and cook for a further 3–5 minutes until that has disappeared too. Season with salt and pepper to taste and serve.

SERVED 4 AS A SIDE DISH WITH NO LEFTOVERS!

8 shallots, peeled and quartered, leaving the root-end on so they don't fall apart

3 parsnips, peeled, and cut into finger-sized pieces

Glug of olive oil

A good squeeze of runny honey

⅓ mug of white wine

1 small glug of white wine vinegar

Salt and freshly ground black pepper

Slow-Braised Chicory

VEGETARIAN

This goes exceptionally well with the Duck and Orange recipe on page 178. It's also a great way to cook chicory if you don't like the usual salad solution.

SERVES 4

1 tbsp groundnut oil

2 good pinches of fennel seeds

A couple of knobs of butter

8 whole chicory heads, washed

1 onion, peeled and finely chopped

Juice of ½ a lemon

A sprinkle of sugar

Sea salt and freshly ground black pepper

Preheat the oven to 180°C/350°F/gas 4.

Pour the groundnut oil into an ovenproof lidded frying pan set over a medium heat. Throw in the fennel seeds and stir them around for about a minute to release the flavours. Add the butter and whole chicory and brown on all sides.

Now add the onion and lemon juice and stir around for another minute. Pop the lid on and put onto the middle shelf in the preheated oven. Cook for about 40 minutes, turning occasionally. Remove from the oven, sprinkle with sugar and grill for a few minutes until the sugar caramelises. Season and serve.

Artichoke and Almond Rosti

VEGAN

It is recommended that you do not make this dish while on a skiing holiday or you are in danger of being pushed out of the cable car. Experience tells. Seriously though, this is another of those really easy, side-dishy ways of cooking one of the few root vegetables that continues to have a season. Simple, quick and don't be shy about substituting other ingredients.

Serve these as a starter with mango chutney or with grilled fish and a lemon butter sauce. They have a wonderful rich nutty flavour.

Squeeze out any excess moisture from the grated artichokes with your hands and place in a bowl. Now mix in the almonds, rosemary, chilli flakes, lemon juice, flour and seasoning. Divide into four equal parts, gently moulding each one into a thick cake.

Pour a good glug of olive oil into a pan and heat gently. Place the cakes in the pan and slightly flatten each one with a spatula. Gently fry, turning once, until golden brown on both sides and cooked in the centre.

SERVES 4

1 mug Jerusalem artichokes (when peeled and grated)

½ mug of flaked almonds (or any nuts)

2 tsp freshly chopped rosemary

Dried chilli flakes, according to your taste (optional)

Juice of ½ a lemon

½ mug of flour

A good sprinkle of sea salt and a few grinds of black pepper

Olive oil

Bang-in-the-Oven Balsamic Roasted Winter Veg

VEGAN

I really love this recipe and it's a great way to use up whatever root veg are left in the previous week's box. If the vegetables caramelise slightly, you've got it just perfect. Increase the veg quantities to serve more!

SERVES 4–6

3 potatoes, peeled and cut into large chunks

1 celeriac, peeled and cut into chunks

3 red onions, peeled and cut into quarters

3 carrots, scrubbed and cut into chunks

A handful of peeled garlic cloves

A couple of sprigs of rosemary leaves, lightly bruised

A handful of fresh thyme

2 good glugs of olive oil

2 good glugs of balsamic vinegar

Salt and freshly ground black pepper

Preheat the oven to 190°C/375°F/gas 5. Put in a roasting tin to heat up.

Parboil the potatoes for 5–10 minutes in a pan of boiling water. Toss the drained potatoes and all the remaining ingredients in a bowl and transfer to the hot roasting tin. Bake for about 40–50 minutes until tender and caramelised, turning the veg a few times during the cooking time. Serve with your favourite Sunday roast.

Celeriac and Mascarpone Purée

VEGETARIAN

Celeriac, which looks like a brain, is another of those great British vegetables that people avoid because they don't know quite what to do with it. Here is a straightforward example. Don't be too put off if this doesn't become a completely smooth paste. Delicious with tuna.

Place the diced celeriac and garlic cloves in a pot of salted water (to just cover) and simmer for about 15 minutes, until the celeriac is fork-tender. Drain, pop the celeriac and garlic back into the pot and move it around over a low heat for a minute or so to remove some of the moisture. Now you can either blitz it in a blender or mash in the pot to a smooth paste before folding through the butter and mascarpone. Season and serve.

SERVES 4 AS A SIDE DISH

1 celeriac, rough outer skin removed and diced into 2.5cm (1in) cubes

2 garlic cloves, peeled

A knob of butter

½ mug of mascarpone cheese

Salt and freshly ground black pepper

Shredded Brussels and Bacon

If you're vegetarian and thinking about moving over to the dark side, try this recipe using English Soil Association-certified bacon and weep at how much you've been missing out on. It works really well as a light supper served with perfect rice and eaten with chopsticks and soy sauce, with an adoring labrador to hoover up the rice you drop on the floor.

This is also a great side dish to have with game or beef on a cold winter's night, especially if you have some nice gravy on the side.

SERVES 6

1 small bag of Brussels sprouts

1 glug of olive oil

1 pack of rindless back bacon, cut into smallish pieces

3 carrots, washed and diced

Knob of butter

Freshly ground black pepper and a small pinch of salt

1 tbsp chopped sage leaves (optional)

Start by peeling the outer leaves off the sprouts and slicing off the tough stalk ends just below the base of the leaves. Slice the sprouts down the middle and shred them lengthways.

Heat the oil in a heavy-based pan over a medium heat and fry the bacon for about 5 minutes or until golden. Add the carrots and cook for a further 5 minutes, keeping the pan moving. Now add the butter and shredded sprouts and toss for a few more minutes, until the sprouts are tender but still a little crunchy. Season and serve with a sprinkle of sage on each serving.

Punchy Leeks and Goats' Cheese on Toast

VEGETARIAN

Something to knock up during the advert breaks.

SERVES 4

1 tbsp olive oil

2 large or 3 medium leeks, washed and finely shredded

2 garlic cloves, peeled and finely sliced

1 tsp cayenne pepper

½ tbsp wholegrain mustard

½ mug of goats' cheese (that's about 100g/4oz)

Salt and freshly ground black pepper

4 slices of toasted granary, wholemeal, ciabbata (any bread really)

Heat the olive oil in a saucepan or lidded frying pan and add the leeks, garlic and cayenne pepper. Place the lid on the pan and leave the mixture to sweat for about 15 minutes, stirring occasionally.

When the leeks are soft, add the mustard and cheese and stir thoroughly until the cheese has melted. Season the mixture with salt and pepper and pile onto the toast. Place under the grill until the tops turn a light golden colour and serve.

Vanilla Swede Purée

VEGETARIAN

If someone calls you up and asks you if 8pm is all right, and you've
completely forgotten, and it's 7pm already, put anything in the
microwave and serve it with this and you'll get away with it.
Alternatively if anyone dares tell you they don't like swede, spring this
on them and their nose'll grow . . . visibly. Don't overdo the portions as
it's quite rich.

Start by splitting the vanilla pod and scraping out the seeds (keep
them for later). Boil the swede with the empty vanilla pod in just
enough water to cover it, until just tender (don't overcook it – about
15 minutes or so should do).

Drain and discard the vanilla pod. Using a food processor, blitz the
swede, butter and vanilla seeds until it becomes a smooth purée (the
processor makes sure the vanilla gets into every forkful). Add a splash
of milk if necessary. Season to taste and serve.

**SERVES 4–6 AS A
SIDE DISH**

½ a vanilla pod

1 swede, peeled and cut
into 2.5cm (1in) chunks

2 good knobs of butter

A splash of milk (optional,
if the purée is a little dry)

Salt and freshly ground
black pepper

Swedeaphobia Cure

VEGETARIAN

This hearty dish is based on a traditional Finnish recipe. Not much survives in such a northerly climate, so they've made creative use of their root vegetables with much success! This dish is worth trying even if you think you don't like swede (or have frightening memories of it) – it's creamy, slightly spicy and I promise you it's delicious.

This dish keeps well in the fridge, can be made in advance, and tastes great the next day – just reheat in the oven for about 30 minutes.

SERVES 4 AS A MAIN COURSE OR 8 AS A SIDE DISH

1 big swede, peeled

1 mug of dried breadcrumbs

1½ mugs of cream (or a mixture of cream and milk)

3 tbsp golden syrup, maple syrup or honey

½ tsp white pepper

1 tsp ground ginger

½ tsp grated nutmeg

Salt and freshly ground black pepper

2–3 potatoes, peeled and thinly sliced

Preheat the oven to 175°C/350°F/gas 4.

Cut the swede into large chunks and boil in lightly salted water until just tender, about 15 minutes. Pour half the breadcrumbs into the cream and set aside. When the swede is ready, drain it, reserving the water, and mash it roughly with a fork or potato masher. Add about half a mug of the cooking water to get a slightly smoother texture. Now add all the ingredients except the potatoes and remaining breadcrumbs to the mashed swede and mix well, seasoning with salt to taste.

Grease a large baking dish and line the bottom and sides with the sliced potato. Gently add the swede mixture to the baking dish, taking care to spread it evenly. Sprinkle the remaining breadcrumbs over the top and bake for 1–1½ hours, until the potatoes are tender and the breadcrumb topping is golden brown.

Top with freshly ground black pepper and serve with a crisp green salad, some crusty bread and sharp Cheddar cheese. Works nicely as a side dish with fish or roasted meat.

Salad of Chicory and Celeriac

VEGETARIAN

I won't bore you with the construction of this salad – just chop it all up and mix it all together. However, do be sure to experiment with other vegetables like carrots, watercress and black salsify. This side dish goes wonderfully with the Pork Loin Chops recipe on page 122.

SERVES 6

1 small or ½ a large celeriac, peeled and cut into thin matchstick strips

4 heads of chicory, washed and separated into leaves

The dressing:

1 stem of chopped fresh parsley leaves

1 garlic clove, peeled and finely chopped

10 capers, finely chopped

1 gherkin, finely chopped

A small dollop of Dijon mustard

A small squeeze of lemon juice

1 tbsp red wine vinegar

2 tbsp of good olive oil

1 tsp walnut oil

Salt and freshly ground black pepper

Optional extras:

Crumble over some blue cheese

Sprinkle over some toasted walnuts

Apple, Pear and Brandy Crumble

VEGETARIAN

In our garden we have an apple tree and a pear tree. The truth of it is that there is enough fruit on these two trees to keep us in fruit all winter, but I'm not organised enough to store it all properly. Instead, I pop all the leftover fruit in the freezer just as it comes off the tree and make delicious easy puds like this until the days start getting longer. Most importantly, don't skimp on the cream (unless you haven't got any, in which case throw on some ice cream).

SERVES 4–6

The top:

1½ mugs of plain flour

½ mug of brown sugar

Pinch of salt

200g (7oz) cold butter, cubed

The bottom:

3–4 cooking apples, peeled, cored and cut into 1cm (½in) dice

3–4 pears, peeled and chopped the same size as the apples

2 tbsp brown sugar

A couple of splashes of brandy or cognac

1 tbsp plain flour

Pinch of ground ginger

Pinch of ground cinnamon

While you are coring and peeling, preheat your oven to 190°C/375°F/gas 5.

Make the topping by mixing the flour, sugar and pinch of salt in a bowl. Slowly combine the cubed butter by rubbing it between your fingers through the mix. This should form a breadcrumb-like texture.

Add the fruit, sugar and brandy to a lightly buttered baking dish and give it a good mix. Now sprinkle over the flour, ginger and cinnamon and give it one last toss. Even out the fruit mix in the baking dish and then sprinkle the crumble top over it.

Pop this into the oven for about 30 minutes until the fruit is simmering and the top is nice and brown. Serve it up straight away with some Cornish clotted cream and a nice sticky Sauternes.

Jenny's Carrot Cake

VEGETARIAN

We get quite a few broken carrots in our trade and the rabbits outside our warehouse can never keep up with them, so we had a carrot cake competition. We held a blind tasting and this one from our friend Jenny just beat the others hands down! As usual with baking, the quantities need to be precise, so this is one for the scales.

Preheat the oven to 180°C/350°F/gas 4.

Start by beating the sugar, oil and eggs together. Once the mix is even, add the flour while beating all the time. Now add the remaining cake ingredients to the mixture (carrots, baking powder, bicarb, salt and cinnamon).

Line a 20cm (8in) loaf tin with greaseproof paper and smear the sides with butter before pouring in the mixture. Bake for about 30 minutes or until a skewer comes out clean. Turn out the cake onto a wire rack and allow to cool before icing.

To make the icing, beat the cream cheese, butter, icing sugar and vanilla together and smooth over the top of the cake.

MAKES 1 CAKE

The cake:

225g (8oz) sugar

180ml (6fl oz) vegetable oil

2 medium eggs

110g (4oz) self-raising flour

75g (3oz) grated carrots

½ tsp baking powder

½ tsp bicarbonate of soda

½ tsp salt

1 tsp ground cinnamon

Butter, for greasing

The icing:

175g (6oz) cream cheese

175g (6oz) butter, at room temperature

225g (8oz) icing sugar, sifted

½ tsp vanilla essence

Winter Bits and Pieces

There are loads of delicious ways to enjoy the odds and sods that you'll find at the bottom of your fridge during the winter months. Here are a few ideas . . .

Roasting

Perfect for any or all of the root vegetables that are so plentiful at this time of year – just cut them up (the smaller they are the quicker they'll cook) and toss them in olive oil and a bit of salt and pepper. Throw in a couple of whole garlic cloves too. Dried herbs or spices if you like, also (nutmeg, cumin and smoked paprika each work particularly well). Then shove in an oven at 190°C/375°F/gas 5; check on them after half an hour to see if done, and if not check again after three-quarters. Beetroot will take a lot longer than the other veg, so if you have these, start them off on their own before you add in the rest. The veg will be done when soft, or when you can easily push a fork through, depending on your preference. Use them as the keystone for a bigger dish, such as:

- Roasted veg with couscous, raisins, chickpeas and spices

- Fajitas

- Pasta with chunky roasted veg, feta and pine nuts

Winter Juices

All the carrots, apples and root veg that are around in winter time, plus our instinctive wish to take in lots of vitamins to keep the lurgie at bay, make this a surprisingly perfect season for juicing. Here are few of my favourites – all should serve two.

Fruity Rooty

Don't let the parsnip put you off – it is creamy and delicious. Sweet and wonderful, and looks beautiful even before you mix it up.

4 clementines, peeled | 2 carrots | 1 apple | 1 parsnip

Sweet Beet with a Little Heat

This will come out super-sweet, so you'll probably want to add some water. This is great warmed up – the earthiness of the beetroot fades a bit and you can feel all the good it's doing you.

½ a beetroot | 2 carrots | 1 parsnip | 1 apple

Kiss Me Baby (or Maybe Not)

The parsnip makes this good and rich. You won't taste the garlic till the end – and then it's merely a tingle. And great for your health.

1 parsnip | 2 apples | 2 sticks of celery | 1 clove of garlic

Mulled Wine

I love a few of these after a day on the slopes or just on a cold, crisp winter's day. Share with family and a few friends, and you are guaranteed of a raucous evening around the dinner table.

½ mug water | 100g (4oz) sugar | 4 cloves | 1 cinnamon stick | 1 lemon (sliced) | 1 orange (sliced) | 1 bottle red wine

Bring the water to the boil and add the sugar. Stir until it has dissolved. Add the spices, and simmer for 5 minutes. Remove from the heat and add the lemon and orange. Let it stand for 10 minutes or until it is needed, then add the wine and heat very slowly, stirring occasionally and taking care not to let it boil. Once it is warmed through, serve it up!

Acknowledgements

This book is for all the wonderful people I've
worked with over the years.

Extra-special first-class thanks to Gary Congress and Michele Simeon, who between
them did most of the work. Also to Ella Heeks for making it look like I can spell and
for fixing problems so fast I don't even know they happened and which I don't know
to thank her for, but I'm thanking her anyway. And to Jenny Heller, who made being
an author just as much fun as I had hoped it would be and told me what pants to
wear for the photo shoot. And to Emma Kirby who realised I'd need somebody to tell
me what pants to wear and put me in touch with Jenny.

Next up Chippy, my Mum, my children Jessica and Hugo, and my dog Deputy Dog
because I love them all so much and this page is as close to an Oscars speech as I'm
ever likely to get.

Thanks to the Abel & Cole staff, farmers and families who let me use their recipes
and helped me out with all the things I'm not clever enough to do on my own:
Adrienne Mickey, Andrew Shaw, Catrina Arbuckle, Christian Finden-Crofts, Helen
Sheppard, Jean Harwood, Jenny Arbuckle and Radhe Ananda.

Thank you to Cristian Barnett, who took stunning pictures, and Nicky Barneby who
designed the book – quite a transformation from my Word documents! And thank
you to the staff and producers who were brave enough to let Cristian take pictures of
them – especially those who got friendly with vegetables for the camera.

And finally, thank you to the very kind, methodical and diplomatic people who tested
recipes for me: Andrea Frishchholz, Beth Lucas, Clare Perkins, Dan Biddle, Hannah
James, Katie 'Olive' Loughlin times 100 because you tested so many, Rachel Carter,
Rachel Dixon, Simon Johnson, Sonja Carigiet and Steffanie Rupp.

And to you for buying this book and for reading this page!

Additional photography by:

Keith Abel: p.70 top right; bottom right; bottom left; p.114-115; p.138 bottom left; p.167; p.181 •
Rob Barkany/Getty Images: p.101 • Gary Congress: p.196 bottom right • Matthew
Harwood: p.2 second row left • Beatrice Rose: p.70 top left; p.75; p.96; p.138 top right

Index